Bible Encounter Series
SEEING JESUS
Workbook

VOLUME 6 — THE EPISTLES
1 CORINTHIANS TO JUDE

Marilyn Hickey

Marilyn & Sarah
marilynandsarah.org

Marilyn Hickey Ministries • 8081 East Orchard Road, Suite 135 • Greenwood Village, CO 80111-2675

Unless otherwise indicated, all Scriptures quoted in this volume
are from the New Internatonal Version of the Bible.

BIBLE ENCOUNTER SERIES
SEEING JESUS WORKBOOK, VOLUME 6

2014
by Marilyn Hickey Ministries

marilynandsarah.org

All rights reserved

PRODUCT CODE: SJWB6

Printed in the United States of America

ISBN # 978-1-938696-77-0

CONTENTS

Introduction	4		Lesson 56 - Titus:	68
1 & 2 Corinthians: Disc 1 DVD Lesson	6		Lesson 57 - Philemon:	72
Lesson 46 - 1 Corinthians:	10		Hebrews & James: Disc 2 DVD Lesson	76
Lesson 47 - 2 Corinthians:	16		Lesson 58 - Hebrews:	78
Galatians & Ephesians: Disc 1 DVD Lesson	20		Lesson 59 - James:	84
Lesson 48 - Galatians:	22		1 & 2 Peter, Jude: Disc 2 DVD Lesson	90
Lesson 49 - Ephesians:	26		Lesson 60 - 1 Peter:	92
Philippians & Colossians: Disc 1 DVD Lesson	30		Lesson 61 - 2 Peter:	98
Lesson 50 - Philippians:	32		Lesson 62 - 1 John:	104
Lesson 51 - Colossians:	38		Lesson 63 - 2 John:	110
1 & 2 Thessalonians: Disc 2 DVD Lesson	44		Lesson 64 - 3 John:	114
Lesson 52 - 1 Thessalonians:	46		Lesson 65 - Jude:	118
Lesson 53 - 2 Thessalonians:	52		Appendex	127
1 & 2 Timothy, Titus: Disc 2 DVD Lesson	58		Leader's Guide	129
Lesson 54 - 1 Timothy:	60		Additional Study Notes	133
Lesson 55 - 2 Timothy:	64		Answer Key	143

INTRODUCTION

I love Jesus.

When you receive Him into your heart, it's totally transformational. I was 16 years-old when I got born again. I was raised in a somewhat liberal church so I knew about Him but I didn't know I could have Him. Later I went to a youth camp and I learned that you could have Jesus inside—Christ in you, the hope of glory. So I prayed, repented of my sins, and invited him to come into my heart and be Lord of my life. And from 16 years-old to now I can say He has never left me or forsaken me and He is real and He can be real in your life every day.

But, I wondered, how can you see who He really is? So I began to read the Bible and I found that Jesus is in every book of the Bible. This knowledge sparked such a passion in me to get everyone hooked on the whole book—to see him in Genesis all the way through to Revelation. Often we say, "Who is Jesus in the Old Testament?" But He is in every book!

I wanted to get people to see who Jesus is inside them—how the Bible reveals who He is in each book inside them. So I began with home Bible studies. I love home Bible studies to this day. So even now I'm doing a home Bible study with you in your home straight from my home.

Many times we don't read the Old Testament. We say it's so confusing but it's not once you see who Jesus is in you in the Old Testament. When you look at the Old Testament you will see that it divides into five segments. So if we know where we are going, we'll know when we get there. It's the transformation of Jesus in your life.

We will be looking at and we will see Jesus in the Pentateuch, in the History books, the Poetry and Wisdom books, the Major and Minor Prophets, and the Gospels, Acts and Romans, the Letters and the End Times.

The *Seeing Jesus Bible Encounter* is a foundational, cornerstone teaching which came from years of in-depth, spirit-guided study of the Word.

My prayer is that your relationship with our Savior Jesus Christ will be deeper and more precious after you dig in and see Jesus in every book of the Bible.

His Love and Mine,

Marilyn Hickey

1 & 2 CORINTHIANS
VIDEO SEGMENT LESSON GUIDE

INTRODUCTION TO *SEEING JESUS* (10-15 MINUTES):
Paul talks about the Lord's Supper in 1 Corinthians 11. What views about the Lord's Supper did you grow up with in your church? Read over this chapter and set some time aside as a group to take communion together. If this is an independent study, you can take it alone, focusing on His forgiveness.

Watch video segment (Approx. 20-30 minutes). Take notes and fill in the blanks.

1. Corinth is in _____ .

2. In 1 Corinthians we see Jesus as a _____ .

   - Paul is training new converts to see Jesus for who He is.
   - We are holy, set apart.

Paul gives instructions on:

_____
_____
_____

Romans 12: Paul lists seven gifts.

1. _____
2. _____
3. _____
4. _____
5. _____
6. _____
7. _____

   - We are special in God's eyes.

>> **KEY POINT:** Giftings usually are where we tend to have the most success

3. Barnabas was an _____ .
4. Abraham was a _____ .
5. Nehemiah was an _____ .
6. Hosea showed _____ .

>> **KEY POINT:** There are 9 spiritual gifts:

WISDOM, KNOWLEDGE, FAITH, GIFTS OF HEALING, MIRACLES, PROPHECY, DISCERNING OF SPIRITS, TONGUES, AND INTERPRETATION.

Notes on 1 Corinthians 12 – gifts

- Paul talks about the diversity of the gifts.
- Gifts are not to be used for personal gain, but to encourage others.

What is a WORD OF WISDOM?

_____

WORD OF KNOWLEDGE: knowing something you would not know with your natural mind

FAITH: supernatural gift of faith

>> **KEY POINT:** Every man has a measure of faith

GIFTS OF HEALING: there are multiple gifts of healing

WORKING OF MIRACLES: believing for the miraculous that comes from the power of Holy Spirit

PROPHECY: different levels of this gift

DISCERNING OF SPIRITS: discern the spirit behind something.

TONGUES: diverse tongues

INTERPRETATION: _____

- God distributes the gifts as He wills.

> " *GIFTS AND LOVE MUST FLOW TOGETHER.* **– MARILYN** "

1 Corinthians 13 is the love chapter.

2 Corinthians 1:20 – all His promises are "yes" in Christ Jesus.

2 Corinthian 2:14 – Thanks be to God He causes us to triumph!

- Paul is teaching about suffering, but teaches us how the Word can make us victorious in our hard times.

2 Corinthians 12:7 – thorn in the flesh

Why does Paul say it was allowed?

_____

"My grace is sufficient for you."

Vs 10 – "take pleasure in infirmities."

Paul said, "For when I am weak, then I am strong."

Jesus Sightings in 1 & 2 Corinthians (15 minutes):

Compare and contrast the list of gifts in Romans 12 and the ones we find in 1 Corinthians 12. What does Paul emphasize in these two different chapters?

___

How did we see the gifts operate in the life of Jesus?

___

Wrap Up (10-15 minutes):

Paul makes a point to say that all the gifts come from the same Lord, the same Spirit. If that is true, why do you think the gifts tend to cause so much controversy in the church?

___

Spend time sharing prayer requests and closing in prayer.

LESSON 46

1 CORINTHIANS: SANCTIFIER

In your SEEING JESUS Study Guide:
Read through the fast facts, author and setting, and overview on pages 379 and 380. Reflect and take notes.

Jesus in 1 Corinthians:

Paul writes to the Corinthian church to correct and admonish the church. Corinth was a prosperous city between northern and southern Greece. Paul was speaking to both Jews and Gentiles in the church. It is a letter of correction to those Paul loved.

Read the following passage. Paul links the church's body with Christ's own body. Circle or underline words that show their intimate connection.

1 Corinthians 12:1-31 – Spiritual Gifts

Now about the gifts of the Spirit, brothers and sisters, I do not want you to be uninformed. **2** You know that when you were pagans, somehow or other you were influenced and led astray to mute idols. **3** Therefore I want you to know that no one who is speaking by the Spirit of God says, "Jesus be cursed," and no one can say, "Jesus is Lord," except by the Holy Spirit.

> **FIRST CORINTHIANS** IS A MANUAL FOR CHURCH PROBLEMS. PAUL ADDRESSES **MARRIAGE, IMMORALITY, LAWSUITS, SPIRITUAL GIFTS**, AS WELL AS COVERS **THEOLOGICAL ISSUES**.

4 There are different kinds of gifts, but the same Spirit distributes them. **5** There are different kinds of service, but the same Lord **6** There are different kinds of working, but in all of them and in everyone it is the same God at work.

7 Now to each one the manifestation of the Spirit is given for the common good. **8** To one there is given through the Spirit a message of wisdom, to another a message of knowledge by means of the same Spirit, **9** to another faith by the same Spirit, to another gifts of healing by that one Spirit, **10** to another miraculous powers, to another prophecy, to another distinguishing between spirits, to another speaking in different kinds of tongues, and to still another the interpretation of tongues. **11** All these are the work of one and the same Spirit, and he distributes them to each one, just as he determines.

> "NOW YOU ARE THE BODY OF CHRIST, AND EACH ONE OF YOU IS A PART OF IT."

Unity and Diversity in the Body

12 Just as a body, though one, has many parts, but all its many parts form one body, so it is with Christ. **13** For we were all baptized by one Spirit so as to form one body—whether Jews or Gentiles, slave or free—and we were all given the one Spirit to drink. **14** Even so the body is not made up of one part but of many.

15 Now if the foot should say, "Because I am not a hand, I do not belong to the body," it would not for that reason stop being part of the body. **16** And if the ear should say, "Because I am not an eye, I do not belong to the body," it would not for that reason stop being part of the body. **17** If the whole body were an eye, where would the sense of hearing be? If the whole body were an ear, where would the sense of smell be? **18** But in fact God has placed the parts in the body, every one of them, just as he wanted them to be. **19** If they were all one part, where would the body be? **20** As it is, there are many parts, but one body.

21 The eye cannot say to the hand, "I don't need you!" And the head cannot say to the feet, "I don't need you!" **22** On the contrary, those parts of the body that seem to be weaker are indispensable, **23** and the parts that we think are less honorable we treat with special honor. And the parts that are unpresentable are treated with special modesty, **24** while our presentable parts need no special treatment. But God has put the body together, giving greater honor to the parts that lacked it, **25** so that there should be no division in the body, but that its parts should have equal concern for each other. **26** If one part suffers, every part suffers with it; if one part is honored, every part rejoices with it.

27 Now you are the body of Christ, and each one of you is a part of it. **28** And God has placed in the church first of all apostles, second prophets, third teachers, then miracles, then gifts of healing, of helping, of guidance, and of different kinds of tongues. **29** Are all apostles? Are all prophets? Are all teachers? Do all work miracles? **30** Do all have gifts of healing? Do all speak in tongues? Do all interpret? **31** Now eagerly desire the greater gifts.

Love Is Indispensable

And yet I will show you the most excellent way.

Reflection Exercises:

Paul lists the gifts that God has given the church that work through the life of believers. According to 1 Corinthians 12:11 who gives these gifts? Which gift do you believe God uses through you the most?

_____
_____
_____
_____

What does Paul say about working together as the church body? How could the gifts God gives us be misused to create division?

_____
_____
_____
_____

Paul is teaching the Corinthian church to be concerned with those hurting in the church, no matter what position or part they have in the life of the church. How can we practice this in our church life today?

_____
_____
_____
_____

At Pentecost when the Holy Spirit fell, there wasn't confusion with speaking in tongues. It seems the Corinthian church was struggling with how to serve one another with this new gift. Paul strategically puts 1 Corinthians 13 between the chapters on the gifts to remind us they must be used with love. What happens when we do not serve with love?

_____
_____
_____
_____

Paul established the church in Corinth on his second missionary journey

Unpacking the Outline:
See the lesson outline for 1 Corinthians on page 381 and 382 of your study guide.

Review 1 Corinthians 12, 13, 14.

There is much controversy about the gifts of the Spirit in the life of the church today, but Jesus said He left the Holy Spirit as a gift. How can we experience unity in diversity?

How does Paul describe love in 1 Corinthians 13? Sometimes we think of this as only applying to our spouse, but it is how we are to love everyone. Love is essential and He even says "love never fails." How does Jesus show us the perfect example of love?

What helps does Paul give about order and conduct in worship?

Focus: Central Verse / Passage
1 Corinthians 16:13

"Be on guard; stand firm in the faith; be men of courage; be strong. Do everything in love" (1 Corinthians 16:13).

Paul finishes the letter with encouragement to the Corinthian believers. What are some things today that we must be on guard against?

How is God calling Christians today to have courage?

Memory Verse for lesson:

O Death, where is your sting? O Hades, where is your victory? (1 Corinthians 15:55 NKJV).

THE ?ARADOXICAL JESUS in 1 CORINTHIANS

We know the Bible does not contradict itself, so it is important we take time to study and understand all sides of the truth and interpret Scripture in light of Scripture.

In Paul's letter, he states the importance of love, but also corrects the believers in truth. Corinth was a pagan society with a lot of immorality. Think about the context of the Church today. How do we practice speaking truth in love with those young in their faith? With our families? Jesus always did this perfectly, never compromising one or the other.

I saw Jesus more clearly in this book when…

JESUS UP CLOSE:

LESSON 47

2 CORINTHIANS: APOSTLE

In your SEEING JESUS Study Guide:
Read through the fast facts, author and setting, and overview on page 389 and 390. Reflect and take notes.

Jesus in 2 Corinthians:

Paul writes to the Corinthian church from Ephesus and it is difficult to trace this period of time with complete accuracy. This was a time of great evangelistic efforts but also times of trials and persecution. Like Jesus, Paul was willing to suffer for the sake of Jesus' Name so that the Gospel might reach the uttermost parts of the world.

Read and circle words or phrases that signal Paul's sufferings for Christ's sake.

2 Corinthians 4:1-18 – A Ministry of Suffering

Therefore, since through God's mercy we have this ministry, we do not lose heart. **2** Rather, we have renounced secret and shameful ways; we do not use deception, nor do we distort the word of God. On the contrary, by setting forth the truth plainly we commend ourselves to everyone's conscience in the sight of God. **3** And even if our gospel is veiled, it is veiled to those who are perishing. **4** The god of this age has blinded the minds of unbelievers, so that they cannot see the light of the gospel that displays the glory of Christ, who is the image of God. **5** For what we preach is not ourselves, but Jesus Christ as Lord, and ourselves as your servants for Jesus' sake. **6** For God, who said, "Let light shine out of darkness," made his light shine in our hearts to give us the light of the knowledge of God's glory displayed in the face of Christ.

7 But we have this treasure in jars of clay to show that this all-surpassing power is from God and not from us. **8** We are hard pressed on every side, but not crushed; perplexed, but not in despair; **9** persecuted, but not abandoned; struck down, but not destroyed. **10** We always carry around in our body the death of Jesus, so that the life of Jesus may also be revealed in our body. **11** For we who are alive are always being given over to death for Jesus' sake, so that his life may also be revealed in our mortal body. **12** So then, death is at work in us, but life is at work in you.

13 It is written: "I believed; therefore I have spoken." Since we have that same spirit of faith, we also believe and therefore speak, **14** because we know that the one who raised the Lord Jesus from the dead will also raise us with Jesus and present us with you to himself. **15** All this is for your benefit, so that the grace that is reaching more and more people may cause thanksgiving to overflow to the glory of God.

16 Therefore we do not lose heart. Though outwardly we are wasting away, yet inwardly we are being renewed day by day. **17** For our light and momentary troubles are achieving for us an eternal glory that far outweighs them all. **18** So we fix our eyes not on what is seen, but on what is unseen, since what is seen is temporary, but what is unseen is eternal.

> ALL THE **"EPISTLES"** OR **LETTERS** WERE HANDWRITTEN, BUT NOT NECESSARILY BY THE AUTHOR. SOMETIMES THE AUTHOR HAD THE MESSAGE **TRANSCRIBED**.

Reflection Exercises:

Of all the apostles, Paul understood hardship probably better than all of them. In the midst of trials, what does Paul tell us not to do in the opening verses of chapter 4?

What is Paul saying in verse 10? How does Jesus' suffering put Paul's suffering into perspective?

Read 2 Corinthians 4:16-18. What is Paul's conclusion about how we should view our temporal sufferings?

Think about the trials you are facing today. How does the closing of this chapter impact you today and encourage you to persevere?

_____
_____
_____

Paul wrote 13 of the 21 epistles. The ones he wrote are named after groups of people he wrote to, such as the Romans or the Corinthians.

Unpacking the Outline:
See the lesson outline for 2 Corinthians on page 394 of your *Seeing Jesus Study Guide*. Review 2 Corinthians 2:14-17. Paul leads the church into the triumph we have in Christ Jesus. He continually points believers to the work of Jesus Christ.

How has Christ's triumph given you triumph over this day?

_____
_____
_____

Because of our relationship with Christ, we are to be the fragrance of Jesus to others. Sometimes we forget that we are encouragement to both believers and unbelievers by our presence. Who has done that for you at a key time?

_____
_____
_____

Focus: Central Verse / Passage
2 Corinthians 12:7-9

To keep me from becoming conceited because of these surpassingly great revelations, there was given me a thorn in my flesh, a messenger of Satan, to torment me. Three times I pleaded with the Lord to take it away from. But he said to me, 'My grace is sufficient for you, for my power is made perfect in weakness.' Therefore I will boast all the more gladly about my weaknesses, so that Christ's power may rest on me (2 Corinthians 12:7-9).

Who sent Paul's thorn?

_____
_____
_____

Paul instructs the reader to "boast" in our weaknesses. Think about a weakness you have. How can you better boast about it and give it to God, whether it is a resource, an ailment, or circumstantial?

_____
_____
_____

Memory Verse for lesson:
For all the promises of God in Him are Yes, and in Him Amen, to the glory of God through us (2 Corinthians 1:20 NKJV).

THE ?ARADOXICAL JESUS in 2 CORINTHIANS

We know the Bible does not contradict itself, so it is important we take time to study and understand all sides of the truth and interpret Scripture in light of Scripture to understand.

One of the most well-read passages is in 2 Corinthians 12 where we read about Paul's thorn. Review this passage.

Paul states that a messenger from Satan sent a thorn to torment Paul. How does this push our theology of suffering?

_____
_____
_____

How do we reconcile God's protection over us when Satan is allowed to torment?

_____
_____
_____
_____

I saw Jesus more clearly in this book when...

_____
_____
_____

JESUS UP CLOSE:

GALATIANS & EPHESIANS
VIDEO SEGMENT LESSON GUIDE

INTRODUCTION TO *SEEING JESUS* (10-15 MINUTES):
In Ephesians, Paul mentions people who the church are called to encourage. Think about the pastors you have known. What pastor has impacted your life the most and why?

Watch video segment (Approx. 20-30 minutes). Take notes and fill in the blanks.

1. Galatians is the _____ book.

2. Jesus came to set the _____ free.

Galatians 5:16:
- Stay in the Spirit
- Flesh

Works of the flesh
- sexual and religious _____
- character _____
- murder, drunkenness _____

Faithfulness is different than faith.

Rely on Jesus, who He is in you.

Go back to 1 Corinthians 12
- The gifts and fruit flow together.

GALATIANS 5:22 • FRUIT OF THE SPIRIT
LOVE	PATIENCE	GENTLENESS
JOY	KINDNESS	FAITHFULNESS
PEACE	GOODNESS	SELF-CONTROL

3. When they operate together you will see the _____ of them.

Ephesians:
Ephesians 1 Notes:

4. We are seated with _____ and can look down on our problems.
   - Get seated, then you will know how to walk in the Spirit.

> *WE SIT FIRST, WE WALK, THEN WE STAND IN FAITH.* —MARILYN

First: He wants us to rest!

- Adam was first to sit and rest with God. Then he could go and "do."

Ephesians 4:

- Romans 12; 1 Corinthians 12

5 Ministry Gifts:

- Apostle – _____

(Paul broke barriers with Gentiles)

- Prophet – _____
- Evangelist – _____
- Pastor – _____
- Teacher – _____

(Differ from other gifts as they are manifested as people!)

These people build up the body of Christ.

Jesus Sightings in Galatians (15 minutes):

Marilyn mentions that Galatians is all about being free in Jesus Christ, that the Spirit has come to give us freedom.

Why do you think so many Christians still live under bondage and chains of generational sin? Reflect and think about this. Respond in a way that is not judgmental.

Wrap Up (10-15 minutes):

Marilyn emphasizes the importance of sitting with Christ, and letting the Holy Spirit take over before we go and "do." As you look at the fruit of the Spirit, which one do you think is hardest to produce on a consistent basis? Take a moment and pray for God to make it your strength.

Spend time sharing prayer requests and closing in prayer.

LESSON 48

GALATIANS: LIBERTY

In your SEEING JESUS Study Guide:
Read through the fast facts, author and setting, and overview on page 399 and 400. Reflect and take notes.

Jesus in Galatians:

Paul writes to the Galatians about grace and justification. Through this letter, we have further assurance that humanity is justified through faith—nothing less, nothing more. Paul reminds them to be free from the Judaizer mindset.

Read and circle words or phrases that pertain to the grace of Jesus Christ.

Galatians 5:1-26 – Freedom in Christ

It is for freedom that Christ has set us free. Stand firm, then, and do not let yourselves be burdened again by a yoke of slavery.

2 Mark my words! I, Paul, tell you that if you let yourselves be circumcised, Christ will be of no value to you at all. **3** Again I declare to every man who lets himself be circumcised that he is obligated to obey the whole law. **4** You who are trying to be justified by the law have been alienated from Christ; you have fallen away from grace. **5** For through the Spirit we eagerly await by faith the righteousness for which we hope. **6** For in Christ Jesus neither circumcision nor uncircumcision has any value. The only thing that counts is faith expressing itself through love.

7 You were running a good race. Who cut in on you to keep you from obeying the truth? **8** That kind of persuasion does not come from the one who calls you. **9** "A little yeast works through the whole batch of dough." **10** I am confident in the Lord that you will take no other view. The one who is throwing you into confusion, whoever that may be, will have to pay the penalty. **11** Brothers and sisters, if I am still preaching circumcision, why am I still being persecuted? In that case the offense of the cross has been abolished. **12** As for those agitators, I wish they would go the whole way and emasculate themselves!

Life by the Spirit

13 You, my brothers and sisters, were called to be free. But do not use your freedom to indulge the flesh; rather, serve one another humbly in love. **14** For the entire law is fulfilled in keeping this one command: "Love your neighbor as yourself." **15** If you bite and devour each other, watch out or you will be destroyed by each other.

16 So I say, walk by the Spirit, and you will not gratify the desires of the flesh. **17** For the flesh desires what is contrary to the Spirit, and the Spirit what is contrary to the flesh. They are in conflict with each other, so that you are not to do whatever you want. **18** But if you are led by the Spirit, you are not under the law.

19 The acts of the flesh are obvious: sexual immorality, impurity and debauchery; **20** idolatry and witchcraft; hatred, discord, jealousy, fits of rage, selfish ambition, dissensions, factions **21** and envy; drunkenness, orgies, and the like. I warn you, as I did before, that those who live like this will not inherit the kingdom of God.

22 But the fruit of the Spirit is love, joy, peace, forbearance, kindness, goodness, faithfulness, **23** gentleness and self-control. Against such things there is no law. **24** Those who belong to Christ Jesus have crucified the flesh with its passions and desires. **25** Since we live by the Spirit, let us keep in step with the Spirit. **26** Let us not become conceited, provoking and envying each other.

Romans through Galatians: "Christ in you." Christians are different from the rest of the world because God lives in them through the Holy Spirit. Their Christianity should affect the things that they think, say, and do.

Reflection Exercises:
Christians can fall very easily from grace toward legalism. What are some ways you've found yourself falling into this lie?

_____
_____
_____
_____

Paul said he hated his flesh. He warred against it with the power of the Holy Spirit. How does legalism pull us more toward flesh than grace?

_____
_____
_____
_____

Compare the list of the flesh with the fruit of the Spirit. The Lord tells us we can judge the fruit in a believer's life.

Our actions should be stemmed in our love for Christ, not for the outward appearance of things. How can we better discern which one is at work in us?

_____
_____
_____

In Christ we have freedom from sin, the Law, and the doctrines of man.

Unpacking the Outline:
See the lesson outline for Galatians on page 401 and 402 of your study guide. Read Galatians 3:10-29

Why did God credit Abraham as "righteous"?

_____
_____
_____
_____

What does it mean to you that you are called children of Abraham?

_____
_____
_____
_____

Read Galatians 3:28. Why is this such a big statement during Paul's day? How is this just as important in our culture?

_____
_____
_____
_____

Focus: Central Verse / Passage
Galatians 2:20-21 is a powerful passage:

I have been crucified with Christ and I no longer live, but Christ lives in me. The life I now live in the body, I live by faith in the Son of God, who loved me and gave himself for me. **21** I do not set aside the grace of God, for if righteousness could be gained through the law, Christ died for nothing!

The crucified Christ is at the center of our freedom. Paul says he lives by faith in the Son of God. What does that look like for you?

___

NOTE: The book of Galatians uses the term **"FAITH"** 21 times throughout the book.

Memory Verse for lesson:
I have been crucified with Christ; it is no longer I who live, but Christ lives in me; and the life which I now live in the flesh I live by faith in the Son of God, who loved me and gave Himself for me (Galatians 2:20, NKJV).

THE ?ARADOXICAL JESUS in GALATIANS

We know the Bible does not contradict itself, so it is important we take time to study and understand all sides of the truth and interpret Scripture in light of Scripture to understand.

Paul warns the readers of Galatia that we fall from grace when we rely on the Law to save us. Because of the Protestant work ethic, it is easy to think the opposite of what Paul says. List three ways we can avoid living by the Law instead of under the freedom of Christ.

___

I saw Jesus more clearly in this book when...

JESUS UP CLOSE:

LESSON 49

EPHESIANS: INHERITANCE

In your SEEING JESUS Study Guide:
Read through the fast facts, author and setting, and overview on page 407 and 408. Reflect and take notes.

Jesus in Ephesians:

Paul spent a large portion of this book reminding Christians in the church of Ephesus about God's infinite love for them.

Read and circle words or phrases that pertain to the grace of Jesus Christ.

Ephesians 3:1-21

For this reason I, Paul, the prisoner of Christ Jesus for the sake of you Gentiles—

2 Surely you have heard about the administration of God's grace that was given to me for you, **3** that is, the mystery made known to me by revelation, as I have already written briefly. **4** In reading this, then, you will be able to understand my insight into the mystery of Christ, **5** which was not made known to people in other generations as it has now been revealed by the Spirit to God's holy apostles and prophets. **6** This mystery is that through the gospel the Gentiles are heirs together with Israel, members together of one body, and sharers together in the promise in Christ Jesus.

7 I became a servant of this gospel by the gift of God's grace given me through the working of his power. **8** Although I am less than the least of all the Lord's people, this grace was given me: to preach to the Gentiles the boundless riches of Christ, **9** and to make plain to everyone the administration of this mystery, which for ages past was kept hidden in God, who created all things. **10** His intent was that now, through the church, the manifold wisdom of God should be made known to the rulers and authorities in the heavenly realms, **11** according to his eternal purpose that he accomplished in Christ Jesus our Lord. **12** In him and through faith in him we may approach God with freedom and confidence. **13** I ask you, therefore, not to be discouraged because of my sufferings for you, which are your glory.

A Prayer for the Ephesians

14 For this reason I kneel before the Father, **15** from whom every family in heaven and on earth derives its name. **16** I pray that out of his glorious riches he may strengthen you with power through his Spirit in your inner being, **17** so that Christ may dwell in your hearts through faith. And I pray that you, being rooted and established in love, **18** may have power, together with all the Lord's holy people, to grasp how wide and long and high and deep is the love of Christ, **19** and to know this love that surpasses knowledge—that you may be filled to the measure of all the fullness of God.

20 Now to him who is able to do immeasurably more than all we ask or imagine, according to his power that is at work within us, **21** to him be glory in the church and in Christ Jesus throughout all generations, for ever and ever! Amen.

Ephesians reminds us that our faith in Christ should affect our lifestyle, particularly at home and at work.

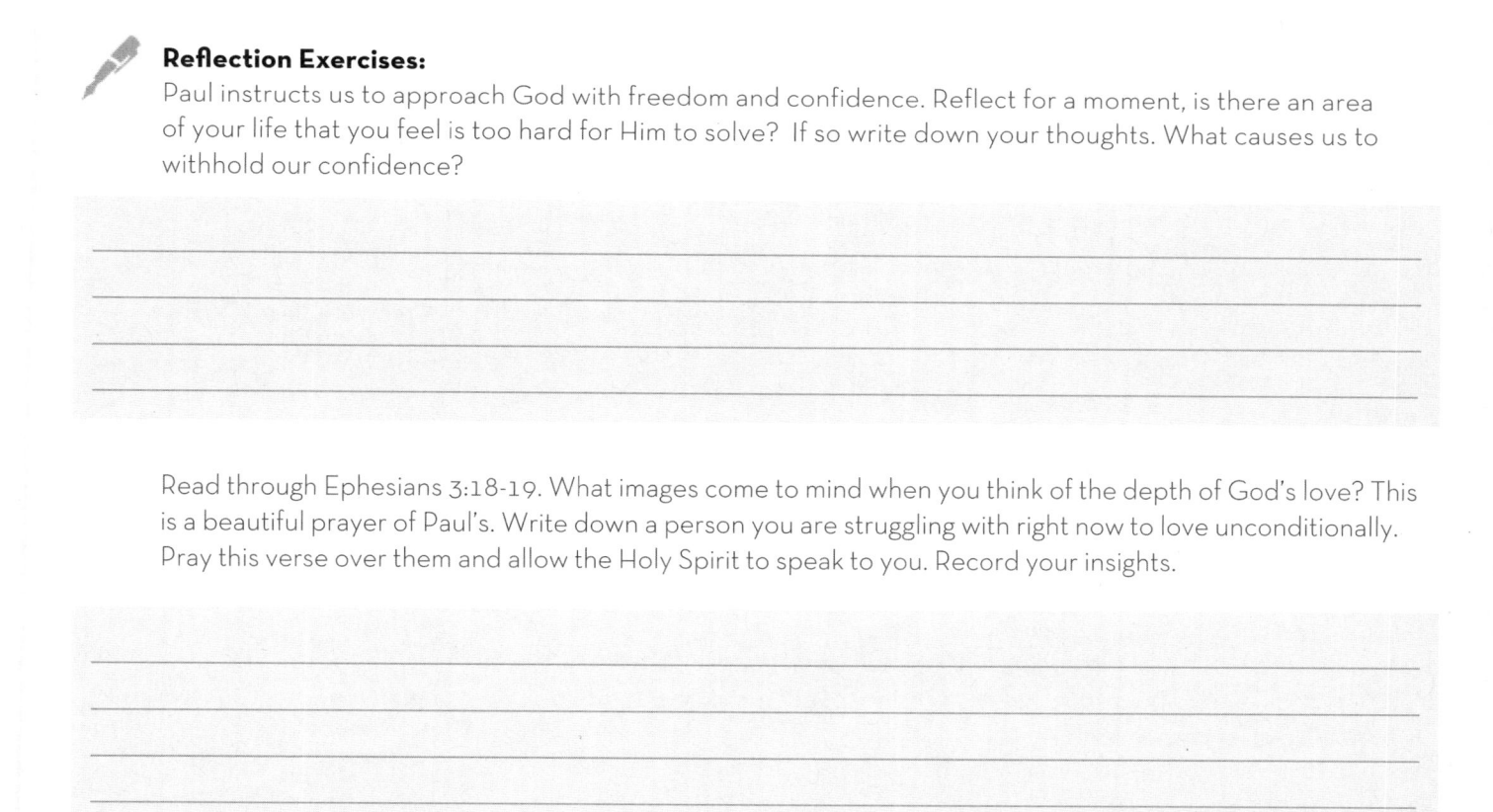

Reflection Exercises:
Paul instructs us to approach God with freedom and confidence. Reflect for a moment, is there an area of your life that you feel is too hard for Him to solve? If so write down your thoughts. What causes us to withhold our confidence?

_____
_____
_____
_____

Read through Ephesians 3:18-19. What images come to mind when you think of the depth of God's love? This is a beautiful prayer of Paul's. Write down a person you are struggling with right now to love unconditionally. Pray this verse over them and allow the Holy Spirit to speak to you. Record your insights.

_____
_____
_____
_____

The incomprehensible love of Christ belongs to the Christian. Christians should reflect on this fact in all of life and in relationships.

Unpacking the Outline:
See the lesson outline for Ephesians on page 409 and 410 of your study guide. Read Ephesians 4 which points to the unity of the Body of Christ.

Read Ephesians 4:1-2. What is the first instruction Paul gives? How does this instruction safeguard the unity we have in Jesus Christ?

According to verses 12-13 what brings unity within the Body of Christ?

Note: Ephesians is one of the prison epistles written while Paul was imprisoned in Rome.

Focus: Central Verse / Passage
Ephesians 2:19-20
Consequently, you are no longer foreigners and strangers, but fellow citizens with God's people and also members of his household, **20** Built on the foundation of the apostles and prophets, with Christ Jesus himself as the chief cornerstone.

Memory Verse for lesson:
In Him also we have obtained an inheritance, being predestined according to the purpose of Him who works all things according to the counsel of His will (Ephesians 1:11NKJV).

THE ?ARADOXICAL JESUS in EPHESIANS

We know the Bible does not contradict itself, so it is important we take time to study and understand all sides of the truth and interpret Scripture in light of Scripture to understand.

Scripture seems to acknowledge a tension between a reality of unity through the work of Jesus Christ, but also that we are to attain to a maturity of unity as an outward witness. How do we live with both tensions and help be the answer to Jesus' prayer, "I pray Lord, that they would be One, as You and I are One."?

I saw Jesus more clearly in this book when...

JESUS UP CLOSE:

PHILIPPIANS & COLOSSIANS
VIDEO SEGMENT LESSON GUIDE

INTRODUCTION TO *SEEING JESUS* (10-15 MINUTES):
Paul talks about the importance of focusing your mind on Christ. What are some patterns of thinking you find yourself falling into that discourage you? Find a verse in Philippians and Colossians that will lift your mind to Christ and write it down.

PHILIPPIANS

Corinthians and Philippians says, "we have the mind of Christ."

1. We need to know how to _____ .

Philippians 1:9:

- In Revelation it says, the Ephesian church lost their first love, Jesus Christ.
- "What they [Ephesian church] lost, is how much God loved them." – Marilyn

Conduct:

- one mind

2. "Unity brings _____."

- avoid criticism

Philippians 2:5:

- Jesus came as a bond-servant; Paul refers to himself as a bond-servant

   (**NOTE:** bond-servant – man who came to serve for a certain number of years; committed to his master)

- A bond-servant says, "I'm still here," no matter what.

3. Paul sends _____ because he is like-minded with you.

4. Paul calls the Philippians "_____."

Philippians 3:13:

- Get a goal and press toward it!

Philippians 4:11:

- "be content."
- Paul's contentment doesn't depend on circumstances.

5. Vs.13 – "I can do all things through Christ who _____ me."

COLOSSIANS

Jesus – Head of all things.

   (See page 423)

>> **KEY VERSES:** Colossians 1:15-19

Colossians 1:20 – image of God

- He is all in all
- He is the reconciler

We are holding on to the Head, and doing what the Head says.

Jesus Sightings in Philippians/Colossians (15 minutes):

Read through Philippians 2:1-5.

What are the attitudes of Jesus listed in these verses?

Sometimes it is hard to think of others better than ourselves, as Paul says, especially when we may not agree with their actions. But how do we protect our relationships and remain humble?

Wrap Up (10-15 minutes):

Marilyn mentions her "like-minded" friend who prayed with her over the course of the years. What person has God placed in your life who is "like-minded" and encourages you to look toward Jesus? If you don't feel like you have such a person take time to pray for God to bring you that kind of spiritual friend.

Spend time sharing prayer requests and closing in prayer.

LESSON 50

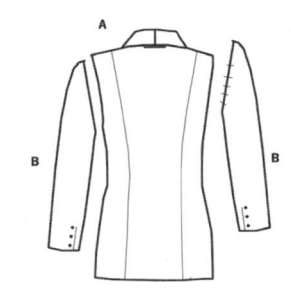

PHILIPPIANS: CHRIST OUR PATTERN

In your SEEING JESUS Study Guide:
Read through the fast facts, author and setting, and overview on page 415 and 416. Reflect and take notes.

Jesus in Philippians:

Paul writes to Philippi with a spirit of great joy. This letter is a thank you as well as a letter of encouragement. Paul had been in jail in Philippi and the prison guard became a Christian (Acts 16).

Read the following passage and circle key words or phrases that speak to Paul's joyful heart.

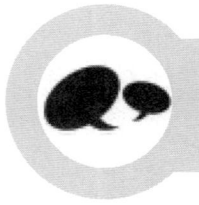

> **PHILIPPIANS** IS A GREAT BOOK TO READ WHEN LIFE IS GOING PARTICULARLY WELL. IT IS A BOOK OF **GREAT ENCOURAGEMENT.**

Philippians 1:1-30

Paul and Timothy, servants of Christ Jesus,

To all God's holy people in Christ Jesus at Philippi, together with the overseers and deacons:

2 Grace and peace to you from God our Father and the Lord Jesus Christ.

Thanksgiving and Prayer

3 I thank my God every time I remember you. **4** In all my prayers for all of you, I always pray with joy **5** because of your partnership in the gospel from the first day until now, **6** being confident of this, that he who began a good work in you will carry it on to completion until the day of Christ Jesus.

7 It is right for me to feel this way about all of you, since I have you in my heart and, whether I am in chains or defending and confirming the gospel, all of you share in God's grace with me. **8** God can testify how I long for all of you with the affection of Christ Jesus.

9 And this is my prayer: that your love may abound more and more in knowledge and depth of insight, **10** so that you may be able to discern what is best and may be pure and blameless for the day of Christ, **11** filled with the fruit of righteousness that comes through Jesus Christ—to the glory and praise of God.

Paul's Chains Advance the Gospel

12 Now I want you to know, brothers and sisters, that what has happened to me has actually served to advance the gospel. **13** As a result, it has become clear throughout the whole palace guard and to everyone else that I am in chains for Christ. **14** And because of my chains, most of the brothers and sisters have become confident in the Lord and dare all the more to proclaim the gospel without fear.

15 It is true that some preach Christ out of envy and rivalry, but others out of goodwill. **16** The latter do so out of love, knowing that I am put here for the defense of the gospel. **17** The former preach Christ out of selfish ambition, not sincerely, supposing that they can stir up trouble for me while I am in chains. **18** But what does it matter? The important thing is that in every way, whether from false motives or true, Christ is preached. And because of this I rejoice.

Yes, and I will continue to rejoice, **19** for I know that through your prayers and God's provision of the Spirit of Jesus Christ what has happened to me will turn out for my deliverance. **20** I eagerly expect and hope that I will in no way be ashamed, but will have sufficient courage so that now as always Christ will be exalted in my body, whether by life or by death. **21** For to me, to live is Christ and to die is gain. **22** If I am to go on living in the body, this will mean fruitful labor for me. Yet what shall I choose? I do not know! **23** I am torn between the two: I desire to depart and be with Christ, which is better by far; **24** but it is more necessary for you that I remain in the body. **25** Convinced of this, I know that I will remain, and I will continue with all of you for your progress and joy in the faith, **26** so that through my being with you again your boasting in Christ Jesus will abound on account of me.

Life Worthy of the Gospel

27 Whatever happens, conduct yourselves in a manner worthy of the gospel of Christ. Then, whether I come and see you or only hear about you in my absence, I will know that you stand firm in the one Spirit, striving together as one for the faith of the gospel **28** without being frightened in any way by those who oppose you. This is a sign to them that they will be destroyed, but that you will be saved—and that by God. **29** For it has been granted to you on behalf of Christ not only to believe in him, but also to suffer for him, **30** since you are going through the same struggle you saw I had, and now hear that I still have.

Reflection Exercises:

What reason does Paul give for being in chains?

Paul's joy flowed from his thanksgiving to God and his prayer life. So often we wonder why we don't have the joy of the Lord. How does thanksgiving and praise grow hearts of joy in our lives? Write down some phrases from Paul's prayer.

Paul tells us we are not only to believe in Christ but we are also to suffer for Him. In what ways is He asking you to believe in Him more?

Paul emphasizes that a Christian's joy has nothing to do with circumstances.

Unpacking the Outline:

See the lesson outline for Philippians on page 418 and 419 of your study guide.

Read Philippians 3:12-14:

Not that I have already obtained all this, or have already arrived at my goal, but I press on to take hold of that for which Christ Jesus took hold of me. **13** Brothers and sisters, I do not consider myself yet to have taken hold of it. But one thing I do: Forgetting what is behind and straining toward what is ahead, **14** I press on toward the goal to win the prize for which God has called me heavenward in Christ Jesus.

Paul gives us perspective on how to finish the race well. What are some of the key takeaways from this passage?

What is the prize Paul is running toward?

Focus: Central Verse / Passage:
Philippians 4:8,9

Finally, brothers and sisters, whatever is true, whatever is noble, whatever is right, whatever is pure, whatever is lovely, whatever is admirable—if anything is excellent or praiseworthy—think about such things. 9 Whatever you have learned or received or heard from me, or seen in me—put it into practice. And the God of peace will be with you (Philippians 4:8,9).

What are some ways we can maintain our joy and protect our mind?

Memory Verse for lesson:
Let nothing be done through selfish ambition or conceit, but in lowliness of mind let each esteem others better than himself. **4** Let each of you look out not only for his own interests, but also for the interests of others (Philippians 2: 3-4 NKJV).

THE ?ARADOXICAL JESUS in PHILIPPIANS

We know the Bible does not contradict itself, so it is important we take time to study and understand all sides of the truth and interpret Scripture in light of Scripture.

Read Philippians 1:15-18. Paul says some preach Christ with insincere motives and that what he cares most about is that Christ is preached.

What tensions come to mind with this, as we observe hypocrisy in the church today and the witness to the world?

How do Paul's words liberate us?

I saw Jesus more clearly in this book when...

JESUS UP CLOSE:

LESSON 51

COLOSSIANS: HEAD OF THE BODY

In your SEEING JESUS Study Guide:
Read through the fast facts, author and setting, and overview on page 421 and 422. Reflect and take notes.

Jesus in Colossians:

Though Paul never visited Colossae, the church began from the outgrowth of Paul's missionary journeys. This book contains some high Christology for the body of Christ to uphold.

Read the following passage and circle key words or phrases that speak of God's preeminence.

Colossians 1:1-29

Paul, an apostle of Christ Jesus by the will of God, and Timothy our brother,

2 To God's holy people in Colossae, the faithful brothers and sisters in Christ:

Grace and peace to you from God our Father.

Thanksgiving and Prayer

3 We always thank God, the Father of our Lord Jesus Christ, when we pray for you, **4** because we have heard of your faith in Christ Jesus and of the love you have for all God's people— **5** the faith and love that spring from the hope stored up for you in heaven and about which you have already heard in the true message of the gospel **6** that has come to you. In the same way, the gospel is bearing fruit and growing throughout the whole world—just as it has been doing among you since the day you heard it and truly understood God's grace. **7** You learned it from Epaphras, our dear fellow servant, who is a faithful minister of Christ on our behalf, **8** and who also told us of your love in the Spirit.

9 For this reason, since the day we heard about you, we have not stopped praying for you. We continually ask God to fill you with the knowledge of his will through all the wisdom and understanding that the Spirit gives, **10** so that you may live a life worthy of the Lord and please him in every way: bearing fruit in every good work, growing in the knowledge of God, **11** being strengthened with all power according to his glorious might so that you may have great endurance and patience, **12** and giving joyful thanks to the Father, who has qualified you to share in the inheritance of his holy people in the kingdom of light. **13** For he has rescued us from the dominion of darkness and brought us into the kingdom of the Son he loves, **14** in whom we have redemption, the forgiveness of sins.

The Supremacy of the Son of God

15 The Son is the image of the invisible God, the firstborn over all creation. **16** For in him all things were created: things in heaven and on earth, visible and invisible, whether thrones or powers or rulers or authorities; all things have been created through him and for him. **17** He is before all things, and in him all things hold together. **18** And he is the head of the body, the church; he is the beginning and the firstborn from among the dead, so that in everything he might have the supremacy. **19** For God was pleased to have all his fullness dwell in him, **20** and through him to reconcile to himself all things, whether things on earth or things in heaven, by making peace through his blood, shed on the cross.

21 Once you were alienated from God and were enemies in your minds because of your evil behavior. **22** But now he has reconciled you by Christ's physical body through death to present you holy in his sight, without blemish and free from accusation— **23** if you continue in your faith, established and firm, and do not move from the hope held out in the gospel. This is the gospel that you heard and that has been proclaimed to every creature under heaven, and of which I, Paul, have become a servant.

Paul's Labor for the Church

24 Now I rejoice in what I am suffering for you, and I fill up in my flesh what is still lacking in regard to Christ's afflictions, for the sake of his body, which is the church. **25** I have become its servant by the commission God gave me to present to you the word of God in its fullness— **26** the mystery that has been kept hidden for ages and generations, but is now disclosed to the Lord's people. **27** To them God has chosen to make known among the Gentiles the glorious riches of this mystery, which is Christ in you, the hope of glory.

28 He is the one we proclaim, admonishing and teaching everyone with all wisdom, so that we may present everyone fully mature in Christ. **29** To this end I strenuously contend with all the energy Christ so powerfully works in me.

*IF YOU EVER NEED A **GOOD REMINDER** OF HOW THE **FATHER** HAS ESTEEMED HIS SON, **JESUS**, READ THROUGH THE BOOK OF **COLOSSIANS**.*

Reflection Exercises:
Read Colossians 1:15-17. What do we learn here about Jesus' authority? List three things below. Then note in parenthesis three things that have been trying to replace God's authority over your life.

What position does Paul give Jesus in verse 18? How does that focus your perspective right now?

How does Paul describe Jesus in Colossians 1:27?

The Word of God helps us to see things in their rightful place, which is with God reigning over all things. Write out a short paragraph here of praise and thanks to God for being the authority over this world and your life.

Colossians is a Christ-centered book, using the word "Christ" 19 different times.

Unpacking the Outline:
See the lesson outline for Colossians on page 423 of your study guide.

Read Colossians 2. Paul takes time to defend Christ's deity. Write out the ways he does this below:

_____
_____
_____
_____

PAUL'S WARNINGS TO THE COLOSSIANS

EMPTY PHILOSOPHIES - _____

RELIGIOUS LEGALISM - _____

MAN-MADE DISCIPLINES - _____

Focus: Central Verse / Passage
Read Colossians 1:18

And he is the head of the body, the church; he is the beginning and the firstborn from among the dead, so that in everything he might have the supremacy (Colossians 1:18).

Look up the word "preeminence" in the dictionary. Write out the definition here:

_____
_____
_____
_____

What are some notable benefits the Body of Christ experiences with Christ's authority? In your own life?

_____
_____
_____
_____

Memory Verse for lesson:

And He is before all things, and in Him all things consist (Colossians 1:17 NKJV).

THE ?ARADOXICAL JESUS in COLOSSIANS

We know the Bible does not contradict itself, so it is important we take time to study and understand all sides of the truth and interpret Scripture in light of Scripture.

Colossians 3:1 tells us that Jesus is seated at the right hand of the Father. We live with a real paradox of Jesus being right here with us but also transcendent, above time.

How do we live with these two real tensions in a way that is practical and allows us to embrace both?

_____
_____
_____
_____
_____

I saw Jesus more clearly in this book when...

JESUS UP CLOSE:

1 & 2 THESSALONIANS
VIDEO SEGMENT LESSON GUIDE

INTRODUCTION TO *SEEING JESUS* (10-15 MINUTES):
Paul started a church in the Greek city of Thessalonica. This was a rough city for new Christians to survive in. They had to grow up in unrighteous soil. What are some of Paul's words of encouragement to these Christians to stand firm in Christ? Write down some of his words or phrases of hope.

PROPHETIC EPISTLES – 1 & 2 THESSALONIANS

writes from Corinth

- Thessalonica was the capital of Greece.

Glory:

Paul talks about the return of Christ

Two revelations:

- Rapture – (second coming of Christ)
- "I believe he takes us out before the tribulation." – Marilyn

See page 428

- Paul teaches us about the rapture of the Church.

1. When Adam and Eve _____, satan got the title deed to this earth.

- The Lord will take the title deed back when He returns.
- This book is written to us, "look up, our redemption draws nigh."

>> **KEY POINT:** God told us to look up!

1 Thessalonians 5:4:

- "Let's keep our eyes on Jesus" until He returns.
- "The grace of our Lord Jesus Christ be with you. Amen"

2 Thessalonians

See page 433

Contrast:

- 1 Thessalonians: Jesus comes in the air; He comes secretly
- 2 Thessalonians: He comes to earth to establish His kingdom; he comes openly
- 2 Thessalonians 2: talks about the antichrist
- we, the church, pray against the rule of the antichrist

- **Lawless one –**

See verse 13: we are his "beloved"

- **2 Thessalonians 3** – practical advice for living

2.   Jesus is going to come back and He is going to _____ and _____ .

Jesus Sightings in 1 & 2 Thessalonians (15 minutes):

How should we live in the end times? Discuss as a group according to the lesson and 1 and 2 Thessalonians.

Marilyn mentions the church being gone from the earth when the antichrist reigns. Think about a world without the church. What further decline in morality could we predict?

Wrap Up (10-15 minutes):

When you think about the Lord's return, do you have fear or peace? Do you find yourself, looking up, around, or down? Am I praying for the salvation of other countries?

Spend time sharing prayer requests and closing in prayer.

LESSON 52

1 THESSALONIANS: GLORY

In your SEEING JESUS Study Guide:
Read through the fast facts, author and setting, and overview on pages 425 and 426. Reflect and take notes.

Jesus in 1 Thessalonians:

One of the major themes in both 1 and 2 Thessalonians is the return of Christ. We see the Second Coming of Christ was on the hearts of his disciples even 2,000 years ago. Paul writes about Jesus as the "returning Lord."

Read the following passage and circle key words or phrases that speak of ways we can reflect our love for Christ and be prepared for His return.

1 Thessalonians 4:1-18

As for other matters, brothers and sisters, we instructed you how to live in order to please God, as in fact you are living. Now we ask you and urge you in the Lord Jesus to do this more and more. **2** For you know what instructions we gave you by the authority of the Lord Jesus.

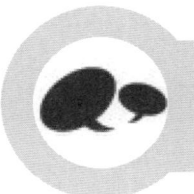

> PAUL STARTED A CHURCH IN THE GREEK CITY OF **THESSALONICA**. THIS CITY WAS **SEXUALLY PROMISCUOUS** AND **HOSTILE** TOWARD LIVING A MORAL LIFE. YET PAUL'S TEACHINGS **TOOK ROOT**.

> *"FOR THE LORD HIMSELF WILL COME DOWN FROM HEAVEN, WITH A LOUD COMMAND, WITH THE VOICE OF THE ARCHANGEL AND WITH THE TRUMPET CALL OF GOD, AND THE DEAD IN CHRIST WILL RISE FIRST."*

3 It is God's will that you should be sanctified: that you should avoid sexual immorality; **4** that each of you should learn to control your own body in a way that is holy and honorable, **5** not in passionate lust like the pagans, who do not know God; **6** and that in this matter no one should wrong or take advantage of a brother or sister. The Lord will punish all those who commit such sins, as we told you and warned you before. **7** For God did not call us to be impure, but to live a holy life. **8** Therefore, anyone who rejects this instruction does not reject a human being but God, the very God who gives you his Holy Spirit.

9 Now about your love for one another we do not need to write to you, for you yourselves have been taught by God to love each other. **10** And in fact, you do love all of God's family throughout Macedonia. Yet we urge you, brothers and sisters, to do so more and more, **11** and to make it your ambition to lead a quiet life: You should mind your own business and work with your hands, just as we told you, **12** so that your daily life may win the respect of outsiders and so that you will not be dependent on anybody.

Believers Who Have Died

13 Brothers and sisters, we do not want you to be uninformed about those who sleep in death, so that you do not grieve like the rest of mankind, who have no hope. **14** For we believe that Jesus died and rose again, and so we believe that God will bring with Jesus those who have fallen asleep in him. **15** According to the Lord's word, we tell you that we who are still alive, who are left until the coming of the Lord, will certainly not precede those who have fallen asleep. **16** For the Lord himself will come down from heaven, with a loud command, with the voice of the archangel and with the trumpet call of God, and the dead in Christ will rise first. **17** After that, we who are still alive and are left will be caught up together with them in the clouds to meet the Lord in the air. And so we will be with the Lord forever. **18** Therefore encourage one another with these words.

Reflection Exercises:
Paul gives some practical advice on how to walk with God in immoral times. What encouragement can you take from the opening verses of chapter 4?

_____
_____
_____
_____
_____
_____

Write down three of Paul's instructions in how to live out a life of brotherly love:

Paul is speaking to the sanctification process, so that we are ready for the Lord's return. According to verse 8, what help do we have? How does this protect us from a works-righteousness gospel?

The resurrection of Christ is the center of God's plan for history and is the basis for hope in the future resurrection of the body. Paul does not say he will be alive for the Second Coming but God gives him understanding about what it will be like. Write out what Paul says will happen.

Paul exhorts Christians in this book to "stand firm," even under persecution.

Unpacking the Outline:
See the lesson outline for 1 Thessalonians on page 428 of your study guide.

Read 1 Thessalonians 5.
Describe what the "day of the Lord" will be like:

Read over 1 Thessalonians 5:12-22. Paul gives some powerful insight in how to persevere until the Lord's return. Write down five key instructions.

1. _____
2. _____
3. _____
4. _____
5. _____

Focus: Central Verse / Passage
1 Thessalonians 3:11-13

Now may our God and Father himself and our Lord Jesus clear the way for us to come to you. **12** May the Lord make your love increase and overflow for each other and for everyone else, just as ours does for you. **13** May he strengthen your hearts so that you will be blameless and holy in the presence of our God and Father when our Lord Jesus comes with all his holy ones (1 Thessalonians 3:11-13).

As a faithful shepherd, Paul prays a powerful prayer over the Thessalonians.

How do we hear Paul's continual heart to see the Church endure through relational strife?

_____
_____
_____

Take a moment to pray verse 13 over someone who is on your heart.

Memory Verse for lesson:

Now may the God of peace Himself sanctify you completely; and may your whole spirit, soul, and body be preserved blameless at the coming of our Lord Jesus Christ (1 Thessalonians 5:23 NKJV).

THE ?ARADOXICAL JESUS in 1 THESSALONIANS

We know the Bible does not contradict itself, so it is important we take time to study and understand all sides of the truth and interpret Scripture in light of Scripture.

Most of us have probably written a letter or an email that wasn't understood in the way we intended. This happened to Paul in 1 Thessalonians when he spoke of the Lord's return. People were quitting their jobs and then resigned to idleness.

How do we live with the real tension of being prepared for His coming but not dismissing what we are called to do today? God does want us to reach as many as possible before His return and to live as travelers, passing through.

___

> NOW MAY THE GOD OF PEACE HIMSELF SANCTIFY YOU COMPLETELY; AND MAY YOUR WHOLE SPIRIT, SOUL, AND BODY BE PRESERVED BLAMELESS AT THE COMING OF OUR LORD JESUS CHRIST. — **1 THESSALONIANS 5:23 NKJV**

I saw Jesus more clearly in this book when...

___

JESUS UP CLOSE:

LESSON 53

2 THESSALONIANS: GLORY

In your SEEING JESUS Study Guide:
Read through the fast facts, author and setting, and overview on page 431 and 432. Reflect and take notes.

Jesus in 2 Thessalonians:

Paul takes time in this letter to address some of the wrong teachings about the Lord's return. We know that this doctrine is still highly debated in the church today, but Paul always points ultimately, just as Jesus did, to be ready and alert.

Read the following passage and circle key words or phrases that speak of ways we can reflect our love for Christ and be prepared for His return.

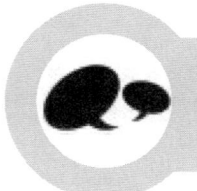

INTERESTING FACT: THE LORD'S RETURN IS MENTIONED IN **23 OUT OF 27** NEW TESTAMENT BOOKS.

2 Thessalonians 2:1-17

Concerning the coming of our Lord Jesus Christ and our being gathered to him, we ask you, brothers and sisters, **2** not to become easily unsettled or alarmed by the teaching allegedly from us—whether by a prophecy or by word of mouth or by letter—asserting that the day of the Lord has already come. **3** Don't let anyone deceive you in any way, for that day will not come until the rebellion occurs and the man of lawlessness is revealed, the man doomed to destruction. **4** He will oppose and will exalt himself over everything that is called God or is worshiped, so that he sets himself up in God's temple, proclaiming himself to be God.

5 Don't you remember that when I was with you I used to tell you these things? **6** And now you know what is holding him back, so that he may be revealed at the proper time. **7** For the secret power of lawlessness is already at work; but the one who now holds it back will continue to do so till he is taken out of the way. **8** And then the lawless one will be revealed, whom the Lord Jesus will overthrow with the breath of his mouth and destroy by the splendor of his coming. **9** The coming of the lawless one will be in accordance with how Satan works. He will use all sorts of displays of power through signs and wonders that serve the lie, **10** and all the ways that wickedness deceives those who are perishing. They perish because they refused to love the truth and so be saved. **11** For this reason God sends them a powerful delusion so that they will believe the lie **12** and so that all will be condemned who have not believed the truth but have delighted in wickedness.

Stand Firm

13 But we ought always to thank God for you, brothers and sisters loved by the Lord, because God chose you as first fruits to be saved through the sanctifying work of the Spirit and through belief in the truth. **14** He called you to this through our gospel, that you might share in the glory of our Lord Jesus Christ.

15 So then, brothers and sisters, stand firm and hold fast to the teachings we passed on to you, whether by word of mouth or by letter.

16 May our Lord Jesus Christ himself and God our Father, who loved us and by his grace gave us eternal encouragement and good hope, **17** encourage your hearts and strengthen you in every good deed and word.

Reflection Exercises:
In between the first and second letter to the Thessalonian Christians, some misunderstandings about the "day of the Lord" circulated. They mistakenly accepted that the second coming had already occurred. In addition, these Christians were experiencing some persecution. Paul wrote to encourage them that the Lord's return had not taken place. From all you have read so far in this Bible study, what is your understanding about Jesus' return?

What have you been taught about the Second Coming? There is much debate about if Christ will return before the Tribulation or after. Though scholars disagree, what are some things we can agree on regarding the season we are in?

_____
_____
_____
_____

If the Lord returned today, do you feel ready? Why or why not?

_____
_____
_____
_____

Note: Paul established the congregation of Thessalonica during his 2nd missionary journey.

Unpacking the Outline:
See the lesson outline for 2 Thessalonians on page 434 of your *Seeing Jesus Study Guide*.
Read 2 Thessalonians 3. Paul transitions here to asking for prayer for his work and reassures believers that God is faithful.

What words of reassurance does Paul give in 2 Thessalonians 3:3, 4? How does this stir hope for us to persevere?

_____
_____
_____
_____

In 2 Thessalonians 3:6, Paul gives a harsh word to disassociate from certain "brothers." What is his concern?

_____
_____
_____
_____

What are the dangers of idleness?

Focus: Central Verse / Passage
2 Thessalonians 1:3, 4

We ought always to thank God for you, brothers and sisters, and rightly so, because your faith is growing more and more, and the love all of you have for one another is increasing. **4** Therefore, among God's churches we boast about your perseverance and faith in all the persecutions and trials you are enduring (2 Thessalonians 1:3, 4).

Paul takes time to commend and thank this body of believers for their love for one another, which was an answer to his prayers. When was the last time you took time to thank a fellow brother or sister for enduring through trials? Write down someone who has persevered under great opposition that you want to thank.

Even though the false teaching was circulating, Paul still says he boasts about the believers to others. Encouragement is such an important part of our faith. Who in your life has shown you the gift of encouragement? How did it help you persevere during a time of testing?

Memory Verse for lesson:
Now may our Lord Jesus Christ Himself, and our God and Father, who has loved us and given us everlasting consolation and good hope by grace,17 comfort your hearts and establish you in every good word and work (2 Thessalonians 2:16&17 NKJV).

THE ?ARADOXICAL JESUS in 2 THESSALONIANS

We know the Bible does not contradict itself, so it is important we take time to study and understand all sides of the truth and interpret Scripture in light of Scripture.

Paul ends the letter giving a harsh word about disciplining a brother. How do we confront in love, but yet not condemn (Romans 8:1)? Can you give an example when an older brother or sister in the faith showed you the proper balance of discipline?

I saw Jesus more clearly in this book when...

JESUS UP CLOSE:

1 & 2 TIMOTHY, TITUS
VIDEO SEGMENT LESSON GUIDE

INTRODUCTION TO *SEEING JESUS* (10-15 MINUTES):
Paul was a pastor to pastors. When you think of your pastor, what roles is he called to fulfill as a pastor? What makes a pastor effective in ministry?

Watch video segment (Approx. 20-30 minutes). Take notes and fill in the blanks.

Jesus shows us how to behave in the church.

1 Timothy - Jesus is the Counselor and the Good Shepherd

- shows us how to live in our daily lives and support one another

1. Timothy is really Paul's spiritual _____ Paul leads him to the Lord.

- Paul is constantly mentoring people.

> " *WE NEVER REALLY ARRIVE* - **MARILYN** "

2. 1 and 2 Timothy and Titus - we see _____ .

Example: 3 Hebrew children

- Will we be faithful when we feel our faith has failed?

>> **KEY POINT:** STAY FAITHFUL!

5 Points of Faith:

1 Timothy 1:15 - _____

1 Timothy 3 - _____

1 Timothy 4:3 - _____

2 Timothy 2:11 - _____

Titus 1:9 - _____

2 Timothy 4:6 - _____

>> **KEY POINT:** Be a soldier, be an athlete, be a farmer...DO THE RIGHT THING!

- Sometimes a servant suffers.

3. 1 & 2 Timothy can _____ us, and mentors tell you the _____

58

Titus

Notes:

_____
_____
_____
_____
_____

- Means "nurse", one who rears.
- Paul gives instructions on a difficult church

See page 451

>> *KEY POINT:* The book of Titus tells you how to pastor: older saints, younger saints, slaves, and problem people

Hebrews 5:14 -

4. Difficult people can push you to get into the word and get new _____ and knowledge.

Jesus Sightings in Pastoral Epistle (15 minutes):

Marilyn mentions the truth that we all have dealt with difficult people in church settings. Think of a time when you felt called to help a difficult person. Did you share God's truth with them? How did God lead you in the relationship?

Wrap Up (10-15 minutes):

Paul mentored many believers in the established churches. What are some areas that you would like to grow in as a believer? Can you think of a resource or a person to seek out? Share and discuss.

Spend time sharing prayer requests and closing in prayer.

LESSON 54

1 TIMOTHY: COUNSELOR

In your SEEING JESUS Study Guide:
Read through the fast facts, author and setting, and overview on page 437 and 438. Reflect and take notes.

Jesus in 1 Timothy:

Paul now moves into writing personal epistles to individuals, not local congregations. Timothy was one of Paul's closest friends. 1 Timothy is considered one of the pastoral epistles.

Read the following passage and circle key words or phrases that speak of ways we can remain faithful to Jesus' truth.

1 Timothy 6:1-21

All who are under the yoke of slavery should consider their masters worthy of full respect, so that God's name and our teaching may not be slandered. **2** Those who have believing masters should not show them disrespect just because they are fellow believers. Instead, they should serve them even better because their masters are dear to them as fellow believers and are devoted to the welfare of their slaves.

False Teachers and the Love of Money

These are the things you are to teach and insist on. **3** If anyone teaches otherwise and does not agree to the sound instruction of our Lord Jesus Christ and to godly teaching, **4** they are conceited and understand nothing. They have an unhealthy interest in controversies and quarrels about words that result in envy, strife, malicious talk, evil suspicions **5** and constant friction between people of corrupt mind, who have been robbed of the truth and who think that godliness is a means to financial gain.

6 But godliness with contentment is great gain. **7** For we brought nothing into the world, and we can take nothing out of it. **8** But if we have food and clothing, we will be content with that. **9** Those who want to get rich fall into temptation and a trap and into many foolish and harmful desires that plunge people into ruin and destruction. **10** For the love of money is a root of all kinds of evil. Some people, eager for money, have wandered from the faith and pierced themselves with many griefs.

Final Charge to Timothy

11 But you, man of God, flee from all this, and pursue righteousness, godliness, faith, love, endurance and gentleness. **12** Fight the good fight of the faith. Take hold of the eternal life to which you were called when you made your good confession in the presence of many witnesses. **13** In the sight of God, who gives life to everything, and of Christ Jesus, who while testifying before Pontius Pilate made the good confession, I charge you **14** to keep this command without spot or blame until the appearing of our Lord Jesus Christ, **15** which God will bring about in his own time—God, the blessed and only Ruler, the King of kings and Lord of lords, **16** who alone is immortal and who lives in unapproachable light, whom no one has seen or can see. To him be honor and might forever. Amen.

17 Command those who are rich in this present world not to be arrogant nor to put their hope in wealth, which is so uncertain, but to put their hope in God, who richly provides us with everything for our enjoyment. **18** Command them to do good, to be rich in good deeds, and to be generous and willing to share. **19** In this way they will lay up treasure for themselves as a firm foundation for the coming age, so that they may take hold of the life that is truly life.

20 Timothy, guard what has been entrusted to your care. Turn away from godless chatter and the opposing ideas of what is falsely called knowledge, **21** which some have professed and in so doing have departed from the faith.

Grace be with you all.

TIMOTHY MINISTERED WITH PAUL AT THESSALONICA, BEREA, TROAS, CORINTH, EPHESUS, AND ROME.

Reflection Exercises:

Paul charges Timothy to fight the good fight. What battles do we face today to maintain our Christian walk?

Many churches have mentoring programs, where more seasoned believers encourage those younger in their faith. Paul mentored young Timothy as a committed brother in Christ. How has God used a more experienced Christian to help you through a difficult situation? How have you helped someone younger in their faith than you?

Paul is teaching Timothy how to guard the flock with care. What are some of the ways a pastor's flock can become vulnerable to attack?

_____
_____

DON'T LET ANYONE LOOK DOWN ON YOU BECAUSE YOU ARE YOUNG, BUT SET AN EXAMPLE FOR THE BELIEVERS IN SPEECH, IN CONDUCT, IN LOVE, IN FAITH AND IN PURITY. **– 1 TIMOTHY 4:12**

Unpacking the Outline:
See the lesson outline for 1 Timothy on page 440 of your study guide.

TIMOTHY HAD THE RESPONSIBILITY TO DO THE FOLLOWING:

- appoint elders
- correct doctrine
- exercise spiritual gifts

Paul laid out the important responsibility to his friend Timothy.
Read over 1 Timothy 3 and the requirements of leadership for church officers. List some of them below:

1. _____
2. _____
3. _____

Why do you think these requirements are essential for those serving in leadership?

_____
_____
_____
_____

Focus: Central Verse / Passage
Read 1 Timothy 2:15 and 1 Timothy 3:16.

What do these two verses teach about Jesus?

_____
_____
_____
_____

How does Paul reflect Jesus to Timothy?

_____
_____
_____

Memory Verse for lesson:

Therefore I exhort first of all that supplications, prayers, intercessions, and giving of thanks be made for all men, **2** for kings and all who are in authority, that we may lead a quiet and peaceable life in all godliness and reverence. **3** For this is good and acceptable in the sight of God our Savior, **4** who desires all men to be saved and to come to the knowledge of the truth (1 Timothy 2:1-4 NKJV).

THE ?ARADOXICAL JESUS in 1 TIMOTHY

We know the Bible does not contradict itself, so it is important we take time to study and understand all sides of the truth and interpret Scripture in light of Scripture.

1 Timothy 2:5 states clearly, "There is only one God." We have to live with this truth as we embrace the Trinity. Let's suppose you were sitting across the table from a Muslim at a dinner party. The topic of faith came up and this Muslim co-worker makes a statement about Christianity not being a monotheistic faith. How would you respond about God's oneness?

_____
_____
_____
_____

JESUS UP CLOSE:

I saw Jesus more clearly in this book when...

_____
_____
_____

LESSON 55

2 TIMOTHY: TEACHER

In your SEEING JESUS Study Guide:
Read through the fast facts, author and setting, and overview on page 443 and 444. Reflect and take notes.

Jesus in 2 Timothy:

By the time Paul wrote 2 Timothy, he was in prison. Persecution was spreading, and Paul wrote to encourage Timothy to remain faithful. Read the following passage and circle key words or phrases that speak of ways we can persevere in our faith in Jesus Christ.

2 Timothy 1:1-18

Paul, an apostle of Christ Jesus by the will of God, in keeping with the promise of life that is in Christ Jesus,

2 To Timothy, my dear son:

Grace, mercy and peace from God the Father and Christ Jesus our Lord.

> **SECOND TIMOTHY** WAS THE LAST LETTER WHICH PAUL WROTE BEFORE HIS **EXECUTION**.

Thanksgiving

3 I thank God, whom I serve, as my ancestors did, with a clear conscience, as night and day I constantly remember you in my prayers. **4** Recalling your tears, I long to see you, so that I may be filled with joy. **5** I am reminded of your sincere faith, which first lived in your grandmother Lois and in your mother Eunice and, I am persuaded, now lives in you also.

Appeal for Loyalty to Paul and the Gospel

6 For this reason I remind you to fan into flame the gift of God, which is in you through the laying on of my hands. **7** For the Spirit God gave us does not make us timid, but gives us power, love and self-discipline. **8** So do not be ashamed of the testimony about our Lord or of me his prisoner. Rather, join with me in suffering for the gospel, by the power of God. **9** He has saved us and called us to a holy life—not because of anything we have done but because of his own purpose and grace. This grace was given us in Christ Jesus before the beginning of time, **10** but it has now been revealed through the appearing of our Savior, Christ Jesus, who has destroyed death and has brought life and immortality to light through the gospel. **11** And of this gospel I was appointed a herald and an apostle and a teacher. **12** That is why I am suffering as I am. Yet this is no cause for shame, because I know whom I have believed, and am convinced that he is able to guard what I have entrusted to him until that day.

13 What you heard from me, keep as the pattern of sound teaching, with faith and love in Christ Jesus. **14** Guard the good deposit that was entrusted to you—guard it with the help of the Holy Spirit who lives in us.

Examples of Disloyalty and Loyalty

15 You know that everyone in the province of Asia has deserted me, including Phygelus and Hermogenes.

16 May the Lord show mercy to the household of Onesiphorus, because he often refreshed me and was not ashamed of my chains. **17** On the contrary, when he was in Rome, he searched hard for me until he found me. **18** May the Lord grant that he will find mercy from the Lord on that day! You know very well in how many ways he helped me in Ephesus.

Reflection Exercises:

Paul exhorts Timothy to not be ashamed of his testimony or of Paul being a prisoner. What might the world say when Christians encounter suffering?

At this time, Rome had made Christianity illegal and Paul knew this anti-Christ sentiment would spread to Ephesus and impact Timothy. Have you ever endured persecution for your faith?

What does the Spirit of God equip us with?

_____
_____
_____
_____

Paul calls Timothy a "good" soldier of Jesus Christ (2 Timothy 2:3).

Unpacking the Outline:
See the lesson outline for 2 Timothy on page 445 and 446 of your study guide. Paul has a whole list of words of encouragement for Timothy. Look up the following verses and write out the word of encouragement Paul gives to his friend Timothy.

2 Timothy 2:1 _____

2 Timothy 2:3 _____

2 Timothy 2:5 _____

2 Timothy 2:22 _____

2 Timothy 4:15 _____

Focus: Central Verse / Passage
Review 2 Timothy and write corresponding verse that matches the description:

The faithful steward _____

The courageous soldier _____

The careful athlete _____

The persevering farmer _____

The diligent worker _____

The clean vessel _____

Memory Verse for lesson:
All Scripture is given by inspiration of God, and is profitable for doctrine, for reproof, for correction, for instruction in righteousness (2 Timothy 3:16 NKJV).

THE ?ARADOXICAL JESUS in 2 TIMOTHY

We know the Bible does not contradict itself, so it is important we take time to study and understand all sides of the truth and interpret Scripture in light of Scripture.

Paul reminds Timothy through this book that his death is imminent. Though Paul speaks of God rescuing him from the "lion's mouth" after his trial (2 Timothy 4:17), he is aware he will die soon. He knew God could rescue him once again, yet he seems to know his time is short. Does it sound like he has resigned? He seems to expect execution. Do you think that shows a lack of faith? Why or why not?

I saw Jesus more clearly in this book when...

JESUS UP CLOSE:

LESSON 56

TITUS: PASTOR / SHEPHERD

In your SEEING JESUS Study Guide:
Read through the fast facts, author and setting, and overview on page 449 and 450. Reflect and take notes.

Jesus in Titus:

Like Timothy, Titus was a young pastor and a disciple of Paul. Titus' assignment was the Mediterranean Island of Crete and its group of small churches.

Read the following passage and circle key words or phrases that speak of ways Paul instructs Titus to lead the Body of Christ, pursuing the purity of the Word.

Titus 1:1-16

Paul, a servant of God and an apostle of Jesus Christ to further the faith of God's elect and their knowledge of the truth that leads to godliness— **2** in the hope of eternal life, which God, who does not lie, promised before the beginning of time, **3** and which now at his appointed season he has brought to light through the preaching entrusted to me by the command of God our Savior,

4 To Titus, my true son in our common faith:

Grace and peace from God the Father and Christ Jesus our Savior.

Appointing Elders Who Love What Is Good

5 The reason I left you in Crete was that you might put in order what was left unfinished and appoint elders in every town, as I directed you. **6** An elder must be blameless, faithful to his wife, a man whose children believe and are not open to the charge of being wild and disobedient. **7** Since an overseer manages God's household, he must be blameless—not overbearing, not quick-tempered, not given to drunkenness, not violent, not pursuing dishonest gain. **8** Rather, he must be hospitable, one who loves what is good, who is self-controlled, upright, holy and disciplined. **9** He must hold firmly to the trustworthy message as it has been taught, so that he can encourage others by sound doctrine and refute those who oppose it.

Rebuking Those Who Fail to Do Good

10 For there are many rebellious people, full of meaningless talk and deception, especially those of the circumcision group. **11** They must be silenced, because they are disrupting whole households by teaching things they ought not to teach—and that for the sake of dishonest gain. **12** One of Crete's own prophets has said it: "Cretans are always liars, evil brutes, lazy gluttons." **13** This saying is true. Therefore rebuke them sharply, so that they will be sound in the faith **14** and will pay no attention to Jewish myths or to the merely human commands of those who reject the truth. **15** To the pure, all things are pure, but to those who are corrupted and do not believe, nothing is pure. In fact, both their minds and consciences are corrupted. **16** They claim to know God, but by their actions they deny him. They are detestable, disobedient and unfit for doing anything good.

Themes in Titus: character counts; follow sound teaching, submit to civil authorities.

Reflection Exercises:

1 Timothy listed requirements of elders as well as Titus. What are some of the qualities of an elder listed in this first chapter of Titus?

Paul's letter gives us a picture of false teachers. Describe what he warns Titus about? Throughout every age of the church, the call to be alert to false teachers and doctrine is essential. Name some modern forms of false teaching that has tried to influence the purity of God's Word?

What are some ways we can be alert and take time to discern the preaching of leadership?

One mark of a false teacher is preaching for selfish gain. Sometimes a person's gifting or skill set causes believers to overlook the need for character. What is the fruit of good character in the life of a leader?

___

A number of Jews from Crete were present on the Day of Pentecost (Acts 2:11).

Unpacking the Outline:
See the lesson outline for Titus on page 451 of your study guide. Read Titus 2 and note Paul's instructions for the different groups in the church.

Crete was known for a culture of lying and slanderers. How does Paul's advice help to protect the Body of believers at Crete?

___

When you think about a man or women of integrity, what images come to mind?

___

Focus: Central Verse / Passage
Titus 2:11-13.

For the grace of God has appeared that offers salvation to all people. **12** It teaches us to say "No" to ungodliness and worldly passions, and to live self-controlled, upright and godly lives in this present age, **13** while we wait for the blessed hope—the appearing of the glory of our great God and Savior, Jesus Christ.

Paul assures us as believers we have the strength to say "no" to ungodliness. Share how God has helped you to say "no" to temptations that led to ungodliness.

What are some worldly passions that you can identify in our culture today that challenge our self-control?

___

Memory Verse for lesson:

But when the kindness and the love of God our Savior toward man appeared, **5** not by works of righteousness which we have done, but according to His mercy He saved us, through the washing of regeneration and renewing of the Holy Spirit, **6** whom He poured out on us abundantly through Jesus Christ our Savior, **7** that having been justified by His grace we should become heirs according to the hope of eternal life (Titus 3:4-7 NKJV).

THE ?ARADOXICAL JESUS in TITUS

We know the Bible does not contradict itself, so it is important we take time to study and understand all sides of the truth and interpret Scripture in light of Scripture.

> Nowhere else does Paul stress the need for morality and character in the leaders of the church than here in the letter of Titus. How does the church press on toward leaders of deep character without preaching a Gospel of just being "moral" leaders? What truths must we consider as you reflect on the book of Titus?

___

JESUS UP CLOSE:

I saw Jesus more clearly in this book when...

LESSON 57

PHILEMON: COMPASSIONATE FRIEND

In your SEEING JESUS Study Guide:
Read through the fast facts, author and setting, and overview on page 453 and 454. Reflect and take notes.

Jesus in Philemon:

The book of Philemon is one of the prison epistles. Here we see Jesus in the emphasis of grace, paying a debt for someone else.

Read the short book of Philemon and circle key words or phrases that speak to the reality of Christ's forgiveness who paid our debt and how that translates into how we love others.

> **THEMES** IN PHILEMON: **FORGIVENESS** AND **ONENESS** IN JESUS CHRIST.

Philemon 1:1-25

Paul, a prisoner of Christ Jesus, and Timothy our brother,

To Philemon our dear friend and fellow worker— 2 also to Apphia our sister and Archippus our fellow soldier— and to the church that meets in your home:

3 Grace and peace to you from God our Father and the Lord Jesus Christ.

Thanksgiving and Prayer

4 I always thank my God as I remember you in my prayers, **5** because I hear about your love for all his holy people and your faith in the Lord Jesus. **6** I pray that your partnership with us in the faith may be effective in deepening your understanding of every good thing we share for the sake of Christ. **7** Your love has given me great joy and encouragement, because you, brother, have refreshed the hearts of the Lord's people.

Paul's Plea for Onesimus

8 Therefore, although in Christ I could be bold and order you to do what you ought to do, **9** yet I prefer to appeal to you on the basis of love. It is as none other than Paul—an old man and now also a prisoner of Christ Jesus— **10** that I appeal to you for my son Onesimus, who became my son while I was in chains. **11** Formerly he was useless to you, but now he has become useful both to you and to me.

12 I am sending him—who is my very heart—back to you. **13** I would have liked to keep him with me so that he could take your place in helping me while I am in chains for the gospel. **14** But I did not want to do anything without your consent, so that any favor you do would not seem forced but would be voluntary. **15** Perhaps the reason he was separated from you for a little while was that you might have him back forever— **16** no longer as a slave, but better than a slave, as a dear brother. He is very dear to me but even dearer to you, both as a fellow man and as a brother in the Lord.

17 So if you consider me a partner, welcome him as you would welcome me. **18** If he has done you any wrong or owes you anything, charge it to me. **19** I, Paul, am writing this with my own hand. I will pay it back—not to mention that you owe me your very self. **20** I do wish, brother, that I may have some benefit from you in the Lord; refresh my heart in Christ. **21** Confident of your obedience, I write to you, knowing that you will do even more than I ask.

22 And one thing more: Prepare a guest room for me, because I hope to be restored to you in answer to your prayers.

23 Epaphras, my fellow prisoner in Christ Jesus, sends you greetings. **24** And so do Mark, Aristarchus, Demas and Luke, my fellow workers.

25 The grace of the Lord Jesus Christ be with your spirit.

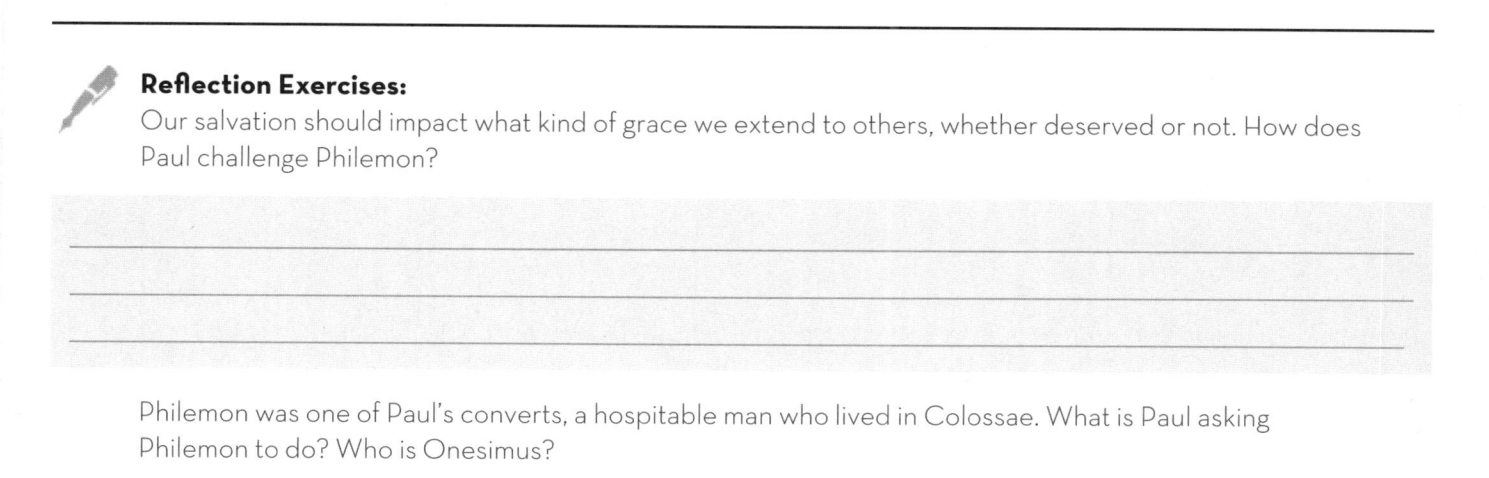

Reflection Exercises:

Our salvation should impact what kind of grace we extend to others, whether deserved or not. How does Paul challenge Philemon?

_____
_____
_____

Philemon was one of Paul's converts, a hospitable man who lived in Colossae. What is Paul asking Philemon to do? Who is Onesimus?

_____
_____
_____

Philemon was one of the prison epistles: Ephesians, Philippians, Colossians, and Philemon.

Unpacking the Outline:
See the lesson outline for Philemon on page 456 of your study guide.

Review the 14 arguments Paul gives Philemon. Onesimus had escaped and traveled to Rome where he met Paul. Providentially Paul leads this slave to Christ.

Most likely Onesimus stole from Philemon and had a debt to pay. Think about the debt we owe to Christ. How should Christ's generosity toward us increase our generosity to those who have wronged us?

_____
_____
_____
_____

Focus: Central Verse / Passage
Read over verses 15 and 17.

How does Paul view this slave now?

_____
_____
_____
_____

What good comes from this runaway slave's story?

_____
_____
_____
_____

According to Roman law, a runaway slave could be severely punished and even put to death.

Memory Verse for lesson:

I thank my God, making mention of you always in my prayers, **5** hearing of your love and faith which you have toward the Lord Jesus and toward all the saints, **6** that the sharing of your faith may become effective by the acknowledgment of every good thing which is in you in Christ Jesus (Philemon 4-6 NKJV).

THE ?ARADOXICAL JESUS in PHILEMON

We know the Bible does not contradict itself, so it is important we take time to study and understand all sides of the truth and interpret Scripture in light of Scripture.

This letter is short but full of importance. Of Paul's letters, it is more like a postcard. But we have three different men in relationship with one another as brothers in Christ, despite varying walks of life. Paul, in prison, asks for Philemon to receive back his runaway slave, Onesimus. Paul was saying something very radical; a slave had no rights. What are the tensions between Paul's status, Philemon the wealthy slave owner, and Onesimus?

How does the Christian faith challenge us to override cultural standards of morality?

I saw Jesus more clearly in this book when...

JESUS UP CLOSE:

HEBREWS & JAMES
VIDEO SEGMENT LESSON GUIDE

INTRODUCTION TO *SEEING JESUS* (10-15 MINUTES):
Do some research on the authorship of Hebrews and the various opinions held by various theologians. Who do you think authored the book of Hebrews?

Watch video segment (Approx. 20-30 minutes). Take notes and fill in the blanks.

Hebrews - the "betters"

God's word is alive! (Hebrews 4:12)

- Author?
- "My opinion: it is Paul" –Marilyn

> " *FAITH WILL PUT YOU PLACES YOU COULD NEVER BE* - **MARILYN** "

See page 460

13 Betters:

_____   _____   _____
_____   _____   _____
_____   _____   _____
_____   _____   _____

Hebrews 11 – Hall of Faith

"It's the big faith book of people."

1. Through faith we _____ .
   - By faith Abel...
     offered with blood
   - Cain rejected ...
     offered by the work of his hands
   - By faith, Enoch ...
2. Enoch walked with _____ .
3. He rewards those who _____ Him.

>> **KEY POINT:** OBEYING THE WORD IS KEY!

- Noah ...

    built an ark by faith

- Abraham, the father of our faith ...

    dwelt in a foreign country, by faith

- Sarah, a 90 year old mother ...

    by faith Sarah received strength

>> **KEY POINT:** "ALL THINGS ARE POSSIBLE FOR THOSE WHO BELIEVE."

Faith lives on! We should die in faith! Keep speaking faith!

- Moses – saw Jesus, Transfiguration
- Samson –

James: Proverbs of the New Testament

5 marks of wisdom – (see page 472)

- **James 1:1-4** – Be a victor, not a victim!
- **James 2** – Live in the truth of what God has for you
- **James 3** – power over the tongue
- **James 4** – keep from striving, coveting
- **James 5** – materialism

Jesus Sightings in Pastoral Epistle (15 minutes):

Review the list above that James warns us about. Choose two of the five marks of wisdom we have and identify a way to live by James' encouragement. Which one do you find is the most difficult for you?

Wrap Up (10-15 minutes):

Materialism is difficult for most Americans, especially as we look at issues of debt. How does our own comfort sometimes become a wedge between us and God? Be sure and take time to give thanks for the material blessings that God has given you and your family.

Spend time sharing prayer requests and closing in prayer.

LESSON 58

HEBREWS: MEDIATOR

In your SEEING JESUS Study Guide:
Read through the fast facts, author and setting, and overview on page 459 and 460. Reflect and take notes.

Jesus in Hebrews:

The book of Hebrews is unlike any other book in the New Testament. Its depth and scope is profound. Many scholars believe the author is Paul, though this book does not reveal who wrote it. The content is written for the Hebrew believers who were tempted to return to Judaism.

Read the following passage and circle key words or phrases that illustrated the faith of all believers who attest to our faithful Jesus:

> THE BOOK OF HEBREWS IS LIKE A **SUMMARY OF THE WHOLE BIBLE**. EVERYTHING YOU NEED TO KNOW ABOUT GOD, INCLUDING **THE LIVES OF FAITHFUL FOLLOWERS** FROM THE OLD TESTAMENT, IS MENTIONED.

Hebrews 11:1-40 – The Hall of Faith

Now faith is confidence in what we hope for and assurance about what we do not see. **2** This is what the ancients were commended for.

3 By faith we understand that the universe was formed at God's command, so that what is seen was not made out of what is visible.

4 By faith Abel brought God a better offering than Cain did. By faith he was commended as righteous, when God spoke well of his offerings. And by faith Abel still speaks, even though he is dead.

5 By faith Enoch was taken from this life, so that he did not experience death: "He could not be found, because God had taken him away." For before he was taken, he was commended as one who pleased God. **6** And without faith it is impossible to please God, because anyone who comes to him must believe that he exists and that he rewards those who earnestly seek him.

7 By faith Noah, when warned about things not yet seen, in holy fear built an ark to save his family. By his faith he condemned the world and became heir of the righteousness that is in keeping with faith.

8 By faith Abraham, when called to go to a place he would later receive as his inheritance, obeyed and went, even though he did not know where he was going. **9** By faith he made his home in the promised land like a stranger in a foreign country; he lived in tents, as did Isaac and Jacob, who were heirs with him of the same promise. **10** For he was looking forward to the city with foundations, whose architect and builder is God. **11** And by faith even Sarah, who was past childbearing age, was enabled to bear children because she considered him faithful who had made the promise. **12** And so from this one man, and he as good as dead, came descendants as numerous as the stars in the sky and as countless as the sand on the seashore.

13 All these people were still living by faith when they died. They did not receive the things promised; they only saw them and welcomed them from a distance, admitting that they were foreigners and strangers on earth. **14** People who say such things show that they are looking for a country of their own. **15** If they had been thinking of the country they had left, they would have had opportunity to return. **16** Instead, they were longing for a better country—a heavenly one. Therefore God is not ashamed to be called their God, for he has prepared a city for them.

17 By faith Abraham, when God tested him, offered Isaac as a sacrifice. He who had embraced the promises was about to sacrifice his one and only son, **18** even though God had said to him, "It is through Isaac that your offspring will be reckoned." **19** Abraham reasoned that God could even raise the dead, and so in a manner of speaking he did receive Isaac back from death.

20 By faith Isaac blessed Jacob and Esau in regard to their future.

21 By faith Jacob, when he was dying, blessed each of Joseph's sons, and worshiped as he leaned on the top of his staff.

22 By faith Joseph, when his end was near, spoke about the exodus of the Israelites from Egypt and gave instructions concerning the burial of his bones.

23 By faith Moses' parents hid him for three months after he was born, because they saw he was no ordinary child, and they were not afraid of the king's edict.

24 By faith Moses, when he had grown up, refused to be known as the son of Pharaoh's daughter. **25** He chose to be mistreated along with the people of God rather than to enjoy the fleeting pleasures of sin. **26** He regarded disgrace for the sake of Christ as of greater value than the treasures of Egypt, because he was looking ahead to his reward. **27** By faith he left Egypt, not fearing the king's anger; he persevered because he saw him who is invisible. **28** By faith he kept the Passover and the application of blood, so that the destroyer of the firstborn would not touch the firstborn of Israel.

29 By faith the people passed through the Red Sea as on dry land; but when the Egyptians tried to do so, they were drowned.

30 By faith the walls of Jericho fell, after the army had marched around them for seven days.

31 By faith the prostitute Rahab, because she welcomed the spies, was not killed with those who were disobedient.

32 And what more shall I say? I do not have time to tell about Gideon, Barak, Samson and Jephthah, about David and Samuel and the prophets, **33** who through faith conquered kingdoms, administered justice, and gained what was promised; who shut the mouths of lions, **34** quenched the fury of the flames, and escaped the edge of the sword; whose weakness was turned to strength; and who became powerful in battle and routed foreign armies. **35** Women received back their dead, raised to life again. There were others who were tortured, refusing to be released so that they might gain an even better resurrection. **36** Some faced jeers and flogging, and even chains and imprisonment. **37** They were put to death by stoning; they were sawed in two; they were killed by the sword. They went about in sheepskins and goatskins, destitute, persecuted and mistreated— **38** the world was not worthy of them. They wandered in deserts and mountains, living in caves and in holes in the ground.

39 These were all commended for their faith, yet none of them received what had been promised, **40** since God had planned something better for us so that only together with us would they be made perfect.

Reflection Exercises:
The father of our faith, Abraham, is given a significant amount of verses in the chapter. Reflect on what you learned back in Genesis. What does the author make a point to say about Abraham's faith in God?

_____
_____
_____
_____

We see from this passage that God's people exercised radical faith, but also experienced suffering. As you read through this powerful chapter, how is God asking you to be bolder in your faith?

_____
_____
_____
_____

Read verse 32. If you don't remember some of the judges, go back and read how they responded to God by faith. Write out your summary.

_____
_____
_____
_____
_____
_____
_____

The book of Hebrews shows Christianity, Jesus' saving work, as superior over Judaism.

Unpacking the Outline:

See the lesson outline for Hebrews on page 463 of your study guide.
Read through Hebrews 1-3, which shows Christ's superiority over all things.

According to the author, how is Christ superior to the angels?

_____
_____
_____

How is Christ better than Moses, who was the receiver of the Law?

_____
_____
_____

The word "better" occurs 13 times in the King James version of Hebrews. He shows us a "better" country and a "better" resurrection. As you reflect on your daily life, how has Christ shown you His way is better than your way recently?

_____
_____
_____

Focus: Central Verse / Passage

Hebrews 3:7-11:

So, as the Holy Spirit says: "Today, if you hear his voice, **8** do not harden your hearts as you did in the rebellion, during the time of testing in the wilderness, **9** where your ancestors tested and tried me, though for forty years they saw what I did. **10** That is why I was angry with that generation; I said, 'Their hearts are always going astray, and they have not known my ways.' **11** So I declared on oath in my anger, 'They shall never enter my rest.'

As believers, sometimes the hardest thing to do is enter His rest. What can we learn here from the history of God's people?

_____
_____
_____

Because of human nature, it's easy to backslide from grace, just as the Hebrew believers. What are some reminders we have to keep us focused on the work of Jesus Christ, not our works?

___

Study tip: For a good review, Exodus and Leviticus are particularly helpful in studying the book of Hebrews. Make an effort to look back at your notes.

Memory Verse for lesson:
For the word of God is living and powerful, and sharper than any two-edged sword, piercing even to the division of soul and spirit, and of joints and marrow, and is a discerner of the thoughts and intents of the heart (Hebrews 4:12 NKJV).

THE ?ARADOXICAL JESUS in HEBREWS

We know the Bible does not contradict itself, so it is important we take time to study and understand all sides of the truth and interpret Scripture in light of Scripture.

Hebrews 12:10 declares that we are "partakers of His holiness." Sometimes our witness is tainted because nonbelievers see our mistakes, not the righteousness of Jesus at work in us. How do we walk in a manner that attests to His grace, yet humbly seeking more of His holiness?

___

I saw Jesus more clearly in this book when...

JESUS UP CLOSE:

LESSON 59

JAMES: PERFECT GIFT

In your SEEING JESUS Study Guide:
Read through the fast facts, author and setting, and overview on page 471 and 472. Reflect and take notes.

Jesus in James:

The half-brother of Jesus, not to be confused with James, the disciple, wrote this letter. James pushes forward great wisdom about conduct and how to live as believers in Jesus Christ.

Read the following passage and circle key words or phrases that illustrated how our faith in Jesus strengthens us.

James 1:2-27 – Marks of Spiritual Maturity

2 Consider it pure joy, my brothers and sisters, whenever you face trials of many kinds, **3** because you know that the testing of your faith produces perseverance. **4** Let perseverance finish its work so that you may be mature and complete, not lacking anything. **5** If any of you lacks wisdom, you should ask God, who gives generously to all without finding fault, and it will be given to you. **6** But when you ask, you must believe and not doubt, because the one who doubts is like a wave of the sea, blown and tossed by the wind. **7** That person should not expect to receive anything from the Lord. **8** Such a person is double-minded and unstable in all they do.

9 Believers in humble circumstances ought to take pride in their high position. **10** But the rich should take pride in their humiliation—since they will pass away like a wild flower. **11** For the sun rises with scorching heat and withers the plant; its blossom falls and its beauty is destroyed. In the same way, the rich will fade away even while they go about their business.

12 Blessed is the one who perseveres under trial because, having stood the test, that person will receive the crown of life that the Lord has promised to those who love him.

13 When tempted, no one should say, "God is tempting me." For God cannot be tempted by evil, nor does he tempt anyone; **14** but each person is tempted when they are dragged away by their own evil desire and enticed. **15** Then, after desire has conceived, it gives birth to sin; and sin, when it is full-grown, gives birth to death.

16 Don't be deceived, my dear brothers and sisters. **17** Every good and perfect gift is from above, coming down from the Father of the heavenly lights, who does not change like shifting shadows. **18** He chose to give us birth through the word of truth, that we might be a kind of first fruits of all he created.

Listening and Doing

19 My dear brothers and sisters, take note of this: Everyone should be quick to listen, slow to speak and slow to become angry, **20** because human anger does not produce the righteousness that God desires. **21** Therefore, get rid of all moral filth and the evil that is so prevalent and humbly accept the word planted in you, which can save you.

22 Do not merely listen to the word, and so deceive yourselves. Do what it says. **23** Anyone who listens to the word but does not do what it says is like someone who looks at his face in a mirror **24** and, after looking at himself, goes away and immediately forgets what he looks like. **25** But whoever looks intently into the perfect law that gives freedom, and continues in it—not forgetting what they have heard, but doing it—they will be blessed in what they do.

26 Those who consider themselves religious and yet do not keep a tight rein on their tongues deceive themselves, and their religion is worthless. **27** Religion that God our Father accepts as pure and faultless is this: to look after orphans and widows in their distress and to keep oneself from being polluted by the world.

Note: James, the author, is referenced in the following verses: Matthew 13:55; Galatians 1:19, and Acts 15.

Reflection Exercises:
One of the hardest things for a Christian is to be "joyful" when experiencing a fiery trial but James tells us to "consider it pure joy." What is his reason for this disposition?

Read James 1:9. What is James saying about position?

According to verse 12, what is the reward in perseverance?

James says in verse 22, that if we just merely listen to the word and not "do" what it says, we can become deceived. How have you experienced this verse to be true, whether in observation or through an experience in your own life?

James is a practical book. He tells us: how to get wisdom; how to control what you say; how to keep from judging others; and how to keep money in perspective.

Unpacking the Outline:
See the lesson outline for James on page 474 of your *Seeing Jesus Study Guide*.

Read through James 5.

Here we have great wisdom for times of trouble and the importance of dependence upon prayer.

What does this passage teach us about financial trouble? Sickness? Conflict among believers?

James understands the power of prayer, just as Paul did. What truths does James speak about in regard to prayer and its role in our lives?

Focus: Central Verse / Passage
Read **James 2:14-19** and answer the following questions.

James says, "faith without works is dead." How is this different than the Pharisaical understanding of outward deeds?

_____
_____
_____
_____

He charges us to live such good lives that pagans cannot accuse us of wrongdoing. What are some practical ways we can guard our witness?

> According to historian **JOSEPHUS**, James suffered a **MARTYR'S DEATH** in AD 62.

_____
_____
_____
_____

Memory Verse for Lesson:

Confess your trespasses to one another, and pray for one another, that you may be healed. The effective, fervent prayer of a righteous man avails much (James 5:16 NKJV).

> " *BUT WHOEVER LOOKS INTENTLY INTO THE PERFECT LAW THAT GIVES FREEDOM, AND CONTINUES IN IT—NOT FORGETTING WHAT THEY HAVE HEARD, BUT DOING IT—THEY WILL BE BLESSED IN WHAT THEY DO.* — **JAMES 1:25** "

THE ?ARADOXICAL JESUS in JAMES

We know the Bible does not contradict itself, so it is important we take time to study and understand all sides of the truth and interpret Scripture in light of Scripture to understand.

Think about it:
Martin Luther described James' epistle as an "epistle of straw." Consider the context of Luther's world, a time when the church was purchasing grace from priests through indulgences. James says if our salvation is real, we should have good works in our lives. What are the tensions to be aware of when we look at someone's outward works? How can this be valid as we discern spiritual maturity?

What is a good safeguard to make sure we are not trusting in works for our salvation? Summarize your thoughts.

I saw Jesus more clearly in this book when...

JESUS UP CLOSE:

1 & 2 PETER & JUDE
VIDEO SEGMENT LESSON GUIDE

INTRODUCTION TO *SEEING JESUS* (10-15 MINUTES):
How has a recent trial helped you to see more of who God is in your life? How did it challenge your faith? Share your experiences as we begin reading about Peter's perspective on trials and suffering.

Watch video segment (Approx. 20-30 minutes). Take notes and fill in the blanks.

1 Peter

- His name is Simon, which means "wavering one."

Peter denies Jesus three times

Jesus told him to "feed my lambs." God doesn't stop using Peter

- martyred

Peter writes these two epistles when he is in a Roman prison.

- Peter, the rock

Page 478: Christian suffering + God's grace = glory

Five types of suffering (see page 478):

1 Peter 4:10

- we are good stewards of grace

1. I have the right-sized _____ to go with the right-sized _____ .

>> **QUESTION:** What is big to God?

Peter quotes the Old Testament, and dealing with Jewish Christians.

2 Peter (Peter is still in the Roman prison)

"Grace and peace be multiplied to you..." –2 Peter 1:2

>> **KEY POINT:** Grace and peace go together.

2. If you are not in the _____, how can you grow in _____?

2 Peter 3:18

False teacher:

3. _____ wants you out of the _____ !

Jude

- Half-brother of Jesus

When we see Jesus in Jude, we see Him as our Savior.

- Balaam, was a seer, but had an experience with the Lord

Notes:

Korah – in the book of Numbers and Jude

- rose up against Moses
- wrote choruses to the Lord

Jude gives us signals to the pitfalls.

- Look to the saints

Theme verse:

- Verse 3, contend for the faith.

4. The setting of all the epistles is _____ , and we are to walk in the _____ .

Apostasy –

Jesus Sightings in Jude (15 minutes):

Jude mentions Balaam, a seer who also prophesied about the Messiah. It seems he did have a relationship with God, an encounter, yet he followed after his love for money. How can our flesh blind us from receiving God's truth?

Wrap Up (10-15 minutes):

We've read through the epistles and have seen Jesus' heart to continue to teach and instruct His church. Some truths about God we have tried to re-invent in the church, or make it more complicated than necessary. Have you experienced ways we've made living out our faith more difficult than it needs to be? Take time to pray for someone who has fallen into apostasy, as Jude warns all of us to be careful to not fall.

Spend time sharing prayer requests and closing in prayer.

LESSON 60

1 PETER: CORNERSTONE

In your SEEING JESUS Study Guide:
Read through the fast facts, author and setting, and overview on page 477 and 478. Reflect and take notes.

Jesus in 1 Peter:

The Apostle Peter writes two letters addressing the scattered Christians who are enduring persecution. Peter, having endured much suffering for his faith, offers great encouragement in this pastoral letter.

Read the following passage and circle key words or phrases that are words of encouragement to anyone who is suffering.

1 Peter 1:3-25 – His Living Hope

3 Praise be to the God and Father of our Lord Jesus Christ! In his great mercy he has given us new birth into a living hope through the resurrection of Jesus Christ from the dead, **4** and into an inheritance that can never perish, spoil or fade. This inheritance is kept in heaven for you, **5** who through faith are shielded by God's power until the coming of the salvation that is ready to be revealed in the last time. **6** In all this you greatly rejoice, though now for a little while you may have had to suffer grief in all kinds of trials. **7** These have come so that the proven genuineness of your faith—of greater worth than gold, which perishes even though refined by fire—may result in praise, glory and honor when Jesus Christ is revealed. **8** Though you have not seen him, you love him; and even though you do not see him now, you believe in him and are filled with an inexpressible and glorious joy, **9** for you are receiving the end result of your faith, the salvation of your souls.

10 Concerning this salvation, the prophets, who spoke of the grace that was to come to you, searched intently and with the greatest care, **11** trying to find out the time and circumstances to which the Spirit of Christ in them was pointing when he predicted the sufferings of the Messiah and the glories that would follow. **12** It was revealed to them that they were not serving themselves but you, when they spoke of the things that have now been told you by those who have preached the gospel to you by the Holy Spirit sent from heaven. Even angels long to look into these things.

Be Holy

13 Therefore, with minds that are alert and fully sober, set your hope on the grace to be brought to you when Jesus Christ is revealed at his coming. **14** As obedient children, do not conform to the evil desires you had when you lived in ignorance. **15** But just as he who called you is holy, so be holy in all you do; **16** for it is written: "Be holy, because I am holy."

17 Since you call on a Father who judges each person's work impartially, live out your time as foreigners here in reverent fear. **18** For you know that it was not with perishable things such as silver or gold that you were redeemed from the empty way of life handed down to you from your ancestors, **19** but with the precious blood of Christ, a lamb without blemish or defect. **20** He was chosen before the creation of the world, but was revealed in these last times for your sake. **21** Through him you believe in God, who raised him from the dead and glorified him, and so your faith and hope are in God.

22 Now that you have purified yourselves by obeying the truth so that you have sincere love for each other, love one another deeply, from the heart. **23** For you have been born again, not of perishable seed, but of imperishable, through the living and enduring word of God. **24** For,

"All people are like grass, and all their glory is like the flowers of the field;
the grass withers and the flowers fall, **25** but the word of the Lord endures forever."

And this is the word that was preached to you.

Note: The sufferings of Christ are mentioned in all five chapters of 1 Peter.

Reflection Exercises:
In these opening verses, what does Peter say about our inheritance?

According to verses 6-7, what are Peter's main points about our suffering?

In our world, sometimes "holiness" is viewed as a bad word and something we cannot fully attain. What does Peter charge us to do in this chapter? Why does he say we should be holy? (See Romans 8:15)

___

Read verses 23-25. What is the "seed" referring to in this passage? What is emphasized about the seed?

___

Peter sets out to build up the persecuted Christian's faith, which is a tough crowd. What words did you underline or circle as words of encouragement?

___

When Peter wrote his letters, he was probably in Rome when the Christians were being tortured. Tradition says that Peter was crucified upside down.

Unpacking the Outline:
See the lesson outline for 1 Peter on page 480 of your *Seeing Jesus Study Guide*.
Read through 1 Peter 2:13-25. Peter has words of wisdom on God's grace in relationships.

What are Peter's instructions on how to view authority?

___

How is a Christian to bear up under unjust suffering? Write a brief summary.

___

Has God called you to "forebear" and endure a time of unjust suffering? Explain a situation and how the Lord built up your faith.

Focus: Central Verse / Passage
Read **1 Peter 3:8-14** and answer the following questions.

Peter challenges us to "live in harmony" with one another. When we are suffering, it can be one of most difficult times to have patience with people. What are the ways Peter tells us we can live toward that goal?

It's one thing to suffer for doing bad things, but another for righteousness sake. What does Peter say such suffering brings?

Peter is used powerfully in the life of the early church, even though we saw him deny Jesus three times. He understood the power of grace.

Memory Verse for lesson:
But may the God of all grace, who called us to His eternal glory by Christ Jesus, after you have suffered a while, perfect, establish, strengthen, and settle you (I Peter 5:10 NKJV).

THE ?ARADOXICAL JESUS in 1 PETER

We know the Bible does not contradict itself, so it is important we take time to study and understand all sides of the truth and interpret Scripture in light of Scripture to understand.

Although it is not a theological treatise, 1 Peter has a great deal of valuable theological truths about God and His sovereignty. Peter speaks of the devil "prowling around like a roaring lion looking for someone to devour." How do we live with this reality, yet not fear the power the enemy is given temporarily?

_____
_____
_____
_____

JESUS UP CLOSE:

I saw Jesus more clearly in this book when...

_____
_____
_____
_____

LESSON 61

2 PETER: THE WAY

In your SEEING JESUS Study Guide:
Read through the fast facts, author and setting, and overview on page 485 and 486. Reflect and take notes.

Jesus in 2 Peter:

Read the following passage and circle key words or phrases that speak to Peter's desire for the Christian to mature in the faith.

2 Peter 1:1-21 – Christian Maturity

Simon Peter, a servant and apostle of Jesus Christ,

To those who through the righteousness of our God and Savior Jesus Christ have received a faith as precious as ours:

2 Grace and peace be yours in abundance through the knowledge of God and of Jesus our Lord.

Confirming One's Calling and Election

3 His divine power has given us everything we need for a godly life through our knowledge of him who called us by his own glory and goodness. **4** Through these he has given us his very great and precious promises, so that through them you may participate in the divine nature, having escaped the corruption in the world caused by evil desires.

5 For this very reason, make every effort to add to your faith goodness; and to goodness, knowledge; **6** and to knowledge, self-control; and to self-control, perseverance; and to perseverance, godliness; **7** and to godliness, mutual affection; and to mutual affection, love. **8** For if you possess these qualities in increasing measure, they will keep you from being ineffective and unproductive in your knowledge of our Lord Jesus Christ. **9** But whoever does not have them is nearsighted and blind, forgetting that they have been cleansed from their past sins.

10 Therefore, my brothers and sisters, make every effort to confirm your calling and election. For if you do these things, you will never stumble, **11** and you will receive a rich welcome into the eternal kingdom of our Lord and Savior Jesus Christ.

Prophecy of Scripture

12 So I will always remind you of these things, even though you know them and are firmly established in the truth you now have. **13** I think it is right to refresh your memory as long as I live in the tent of this body, **14** because I know that I will soon put it aside, as our Lord Jesus Christ has made clear to me. **15** And I will make every effort to see that after my departure you will always be able to remember these things.

16 For we did not follow cleverly devised stories when we told you about the coming of our Lord Jesus Christ in power, but we were eyewitnesses of his majesty. **17** He received honor and glory from God the Father when the voice came to him from the Majestic Glory, saying, "This is my Son, whom I love; with him I am well pleased." **18** We ourselves heard this voice that came from heaven when we were with him on the sacred mountain.

19 We also have the prophetic message as something completely reliable, and you will do well to pay attention to it, as to a light shining in a dark place, until the day dawns and the morning star rises in your hearts. **20** Above all, you must understand that no prophecy of Scripture came about by the prophet's own interpretation of things. **21** For prophecy never had its origin in the human will, but prophets, though human, spoke from God as they were carried along by the Holy Spirit.

Note: 2 Peter was written shortly before Peter's death.

Reflection Exercises:

In 2 Peter 1:5-8, we see the cultivation of the Christian virtues which bears fruit. Summarize what this fruit looks like?

_____
_____
_____
_____

Peter mentions that he can attest to Jesus Christ as an eyewitness, not as a follower of clever invented stories. Why do the eyewitness accounts matter so much in Scripture? Most likely Peter was defending the resurrection of Jesus Christ in this passage.

_____
_____
_____
_____

Peter connects his witness to those of the Old Testament prophecies. All point to Jesus Christ and His coming. What does Peter say to "pay close attention" to?

Both 1 and 2 Peter tackle three difficult questions:

1) How should we live when trials overwhelm?

2) What should we do during terrible times?

3) How should we respond when we suffer for doing right?

Unpacking the Outline:
See the lesson outline for 2 Peter on page 487 of your *Seeing Jesus Study Guide*.
Read through 2 Peter 2 regarding his warnings against false prophets.

This topic is very important today in the life of the church. Peter suggests there are different reasons for false teachers. How does heresy enter into a church?

What role does discernment play in the life of your church? How can we be more discerning?

Peter does mention that false teachers will be popular. Do you think this is still true today?

🔍 Focus: Central Verse / Passage
2 Peter 1:3-4

As we know Jesus better, his divine power gives us everything we need for living a godly life. He has called us to receive his own glory and goodness! **4** And by that same mighty power, he has given us all of his rich and wonderful promises (2 Peter 1:3-4).

As you have grown in your faith, how do you find that Jesus is more and more all that you really need?

Jesus has given us promises for our life we can stand upon. List some of His promises below that are especially meaningful to you right now.

> *SUFFERING IS A MISFORTUNE, AS VIEWED FROM THE ONE SIDE, AND A DISCIPLINE AS VIEWED FROM THE OTHER.* **- SAMUEL SMILES**

Memory Verse for Lesson:

You, therefore, beloved, since you know this beforehand, beware lest you also fall from your own steadfastness, being led away with the error of the wicked; but grow in the grace and knowledge of our Lord and Savior Jesus Christ. To Him be the glory both now and forever. Amen (2 Peter 3:17, 18 NKJV).

THE ?ARADOXICAL JESUS in 2 PETER

We know the Bible does not contradict itself, so it is important we take time to study and understand all sides of the truth and interpret Scripture in light of Scripture to understand.

The topic of false teachers was an important one to the fledging churches because of the heresies that tried to lead people astray. We are faced often with false prophets who we do not know are false prophets. There are some real tensions we need to face and be alert.

We know false prophets from Scripture can prophesy truth, so what should be our test in discerning a prophet?

_____
_____
_____
_____

I saw Jesus more clearly in this book when...

_____
_____
_____

JESUS UP CLOSE:

LESSON 62

1 JOHN: LOVE

In your SEEING JESUS Study Guide:
Read through the fast facts, author and setting, and overview on page 489 and 490. Reflect and take notes.

Jesus in 1 John:

The Apostle John speaks about love in this short letter. He is the disciple "Jesus loved" (John 21:20). This is the same disciple who was inspired to write John 3:16, about God's love for the whole world.

Read the following passage and circle key words or phrases that speak to how experiencing God's love should shape our conduct.

1 John 2:1-29

My dear children, I write this to you so that you will not sin. But if anybody does sin, we have an advocate with the Father—Jesus Christ, the Righteous One. **2** He is the atoning sacrifice for our sins, and not only for ours but also for the sins of the whole world.

Love and Hatred for Fellow Believers

3 We know that we have come to know him if we keep his commands. **4** Whoever says, "I know him," but does not do what he commands is a liar, and the truth is not in that person. **5** But if anyone obeys his word, love for God is truly made complete in them. This is how we know we are in him: **6** Whoever claims to live in him must live as Jesus did.

7 Dear friends, I am not writing you a new command but an old one, which you have had since the beginning. This old command is the message you have heard. **8** Yet I am writing you a new command; its truth is seen in him and in you, because the darkness is passing and the true light is already shining.

9 Anyone who claims to be in the light but hates a brother or sister is still in the darkness. **10** Anyone who loves their brother and sister lives in the light, and there is nothing in them to make them stumble. **11** But anyone who hates a brother or sister is in the darkness and walks around in the darkness. They do not know where they are going, because the darkness has blinded them.

Reasons for Writing

12 I am writing to you, dear children,
　because your sins have been forgiven on
　　account of his name.
13 I am writing to you, fathers,
　because you know him who is from the beginning.
I am writing to you, young men,
　because you have overcome the evil one.

14 I write to you, dear children,
　because you know the Father.
I write to you, fathers,
　because you know him who is from the beginning.
I write to you, young men,
　because you are strong,
　and the word of God lives in you,
　and you have overcome the evil one.

On Not Loving the World

15 Do not love the world or anything in the world. If anyone loves the world, love for the Father is not in them. **16** For everything in the world—the lust of the flesh, the lust of the eyes, and the pride of life—comes not from the Father but from the world. **17** The world and its desires pass away, but whoever does the will of God lives forever.

Warnings Against Denying the Son

18 Dear children, this is the last hour; and as you have heard that the antichrist is coming, even now many antichrists have come. This is how we know it is the last hour. **19** They went out from us, but they did not really belong to us. For if they had belonged to us, they would have remained with us; but their going showed that none of them belonged to us.

20 But you have an anointing from the Holy One, and all of you know the truth. **21** I do not write to you because you do not know the truth, but because you do know it and because no lie comes from the truth. **22** Who is the liar? It is whoever denies that Jesus is the Christ. Such a person is the antichrist—denying the Father and the Son. **23** No one who denies the Son has the Father; whoever acknowledges the Son has the Father also.

24 As for you, see that what you have heard from the beginning remains in you. If it does, you also will remain in the Son and in the Father. **25** And this is what he promised us—eternal life.

26 I am writing these things to you about those who are trying to lead you astray. **27** As for you, the anointing you received from him remains in you, and you do not need anyone to teach you. But as his anointing teaches you about all things and as that anointing is real, not counterfeit—just as it has taught you, remain in him.

God's Children and Sin

28 And now, dear children, continue in him, so that when he appears we may be confident and unashamed before him at his coming.

29 If you know that he is righteous, you know that everyone who does what is right has been born of him.

Note: First, Second, and Third John are three letters that follow John's trademark of love, focusing on: loving God, loving God's Word, and showing love to others.

John warns us to not love the world. What are some behaviors that speak to a love for the world? Compare your list with how a spirit-led believer should view the world.

___

1 John 2:26 is sometimes listed when looking at the ways Jesus was tempted by satan in the wilderness, through: the lust of the eyes, the lust of the flesh, and the pride of life. Which one of these tends to be your weakness when the enemy tries to tempt you?

___

John speaks of the anointing of the Spirit that teaches us, and keeps us from walking in the counterfeit. What key concepts is the Spirit bringing to mind after reading this chapter?

___

John authored: the gospel of John, 1 John, 2 John, 3 John, and Revelation.

Unpacking the Outline:
See the lesson outline for 1 John on page 491 of your study guide.
Read through 1 John 4:7-5:12, which speaks about our fellowship with God.

John states here that God sent his one and only Son so we can live (1 John 4:9; John 3:16-17). Because of this sacrifice, we have fellowship with God. How can we better cultivate the reality and depth of fellowship God desires from His children? What are things that hinder this fellowship?

___

The text says, "we are in God and God is in us." This is a profound truth. How does this speak to our position with God and how much He loves us?

___

🔍 **Focus: Central Verse / Passage**
1 John 1:5-7

This is the message we have heard from him and declare to you: God is light; in him there is no darkness at all. **6** If we claim to have fellowship with him and yet walk in the darkness, we lie and do not live out the truth. **7** But if we walk in the light, as he is in the light, we have fellowship with one another, and the blood of Jesus, his Son, purifies us from all sin (1 John 1:5-7).

Sometimes it is easy to think we can bring God into dark places in our world. His light shines powerfully in darkness. What places have you not allowed God to enter because of fear?

___

How does God's light impact our fellowship with one another?

___

Memory Verse for lesson:
This is the message which we have heard from Him and declare to you, that God is light and in Him is no darkness at all (1 John 1:5 NKJV).

THE ?ARADOXICAL JESUS in 1 JOHN

We know the Bible does not contradict itself, so it is important we take time to study and understand all sides of the truth and interpret Scripture in light of Scripture to understand.

John says that if we claim to have no sin, we have made God to be a liar. Yet we also know that God sees us as righteous because of His son. Both are equally true. How can we clearly understand these two truths without resisting the other?

I saw Jesus more clearly in this book when...

JESUS UP CLOSE:

LESSON 63

2 JOHN: THE LIGHT

In your SEEING JESUS Study Guide:
Read through the fast facts, author and setting, and overview on page 493 and 494. Reflect and take notes.

Jesus in 2 John:

John was a pillar to the early church and his writings encouraged the early church to remain true to God's love and His teachings. Gnosticism was a great threat to the early church, which denied the incarnation of Jesus.

Read all of 2 John in one sitting. Circle and underline words that speak to the importance of both truth and love.

2 John

To the elect lady and her children, whom I love in truth, and not only I, but also all those who have known the truth, **2** because of the truth which abides in us and will be with us forever:

3 Grace, mercy, and peace will be with you from God the Father and from the Lord Jesus Christ, the Son of the Father, in truth and love.

Walk in Christ's Commandments

4 I rejoiced greatly that I have found some of your children walking in truth, as we received commandment from the Father. **5** And now I plead with you, lady, not as though I wrote a new commandment to you, but that which we have had from the beginning: that we love one another. **6** This is love, that we walk according to His commandments.

This is the commandment, that as you have heard from the beginning, you should walk in it.

Beware of Antichrist Deceivers

7 For many deceivers have gone out into the world who do not confess Jesus Christ as coming in the flesh. This is a deceiver and an antichrist. **8** Look to yourselves, that we do not lose those things we worked for, but that we may receive a full reward.

9 Whoever transgresses and does not abide in the doctrine of Christ does not have God. He who abides in the doctrine of Christ has both the Father and the Son. **10** If anyone comes to you and does not bring this doctrine, do not receive him into your house nor greet him; **11** for he who greets him shares in his evil deeds.

John's Farewell Greeting

12 Having many things to write to you, I did not wish to do so with paper and ink; but I hope to come to you and speak face to face, that our joy may be full.

13 The children of your elect sister greet you. Amen.

> *LOOK TO YOURSELVES, THAT WE DO NOT LOSE THOSE THINGS WE WORKED FOR, BUT THAT WE MAY RECEIVE A FULL REWARD.*

Reflection Exercises:

How does John define "love" in verse 6?

Who does John warn us about in verse 7? What are some signs of an antichrist spirit?

In these short verses, John speaks of truth, love, the antichrist spirit, and abiding in Christ. As a refresher, turn to John 15. How do we abide in Christ?

_____
_____
_____
_____

John authored: the gospel of John, 1 John, 2 John, 3 John, and Revelation.

Unpacking the Outline:
See the lesson outline for 2 John on page 495 of your study guide.

Read through 2 John 7-11.

Truth and the abundant life go together. Think about a time when a small lie would have been an easy way to take, but God convicted you to stand by the truth. The truth is a powerful force and John encourages us to trust it as a way of life. How does the truth protect our lives?

_____
_____
_____
_____

A lie always begets another lie and the vicious circle continues to take over. How does the truth protect our peace?

_____
_____
_____
_____

Focus: Central Verse / Passage
2 John 7

Many deceivers, who do not acknowledge Jesus Christ as coming in the flesh, have gone out into the world. Any such person is the deceiver and the antichrist (2 John 7).

Why is defending the Incarnation of Christ so key in the life of the church, even today?

_____
_____
_____
_____

Memory Verse for lesson:
This is love, that we walk according to His commandments. This is the commandment, that as you have heard from the beginning, you should walk in it (2 John 6 NKJV).

THE ?ARADOXICAL JESUS in 2 JOHN

We know the Bible does not contradict itself, so it is important to take time to study and understand all sides of the truth and interpret Scripture in light of Scripture to grasp the whole truth as much as possible.

In this very short letter, John stresses the need for both truth and love to be exercised in our lives. What happens when we emphasize truth without love?

_____
_____
_____
_____
_____

What happens when we exercise love without truth?

_____
_____
_____
_____
_____

JESUS UP CLOSE:

I saw Jesus more clearly in this book when...

_____
_____
_____
_____

LESSON 64

3 JOHN: PROSPERITY

In your SEEING JESUS Study Guide:
Read through the fast facts, author and setting, and overview on page 497 and 498. Reflect and take notes.

Jesus in 3 John:

Third John is the shortest book in the Bible. He sends a warm greeting and John's love for his friend shines through in the salutation to Gaius.

Read 3 John in one sitting. Circle words or phrases that speak of John's words of blessing over his friend.

3 John – Prosperity

The elder,

To my dear friend Gaius, whom I love in the truth.

2 Dear friend, I pray that you may enjoy good health and that all may go well with you, even as your soul is getting along well. **3** It gave me great joy when some believers came and testified about your faithfulness to the truth, telling how you continue to walk in it. **4** I have no greater joy than to hear that my children are walking in the truth.

5 Dear friend, you are faithful in what you are doing for the brothers and sisters, even though they are strangers to you. **6** They have told the church about your love. Please send them on their way in a manner that honors God. **7** It was for the sake of the Name that they went out, receiving no help from the pagans. **8** We ought therefore to show hospitality to such people so that we may work together for the truth.

9 I wrote to the church, but Diotrephes, who loves to be first, will not welcome us. **10** So when I come, I will call attention to what he is doing, spreading malicious nonsense about us. Not satisfied with that, he even refuses to welcome other believers. He also stops those who want to do so and puts them out of the church.

11 Dear friend, do not imitate what is evil but what is good. Anyone who does what is good is from God. Anyone who does what is evil has not seen God. **12** Demetrius is well spoken of by everyone—and even by the truth itself. We also speak well of him, and you know that our testimony is true.

13 I have much to write you, but I do not want to do so with pen and ink. 14 I hope to see you soon, and we will talk face to face.

Peace to you. The friends here send their greetings. Greet the friends there by name.

Note: Third John makes no direct mention of Christ except in verse 7 "for His Namesake", yet we see how Christ's love impacts John's letter.

Reflection Exercises:
What is Gaius commended for?

John wishes good health on his friend, Gaius, which doesn't mean he was necessarily ill. He prays for his well-being and for the whole state of his spiritual life. Take a moment here and write down the name of three friends who are serving God whole-heartedly that you know. Pray a blessing over them with John's words.

There is a letter we do not have concerning Diotrephes. We are not sure why there was hesitancy to offer hospitality. Think about missionaries you know. The ministry of hospitality is very important. When have you been refreshed by someone's gracious hospitality?

Although this letter is highly official, it is also very personal.

🔍 Unpacking the Outline:
See the lesson outline for 3 John on page 498 of your study guide.

🔍 Focus: Central Verse / Passage
Read 2 John 9-11

Diotrephes resisted God's truth. What are some reasons we can resist God's truth?

Sometimes we can resist truth just falling into line with status quo. When have you seen this attitude negatively impact the Body of Christ?

Memory Verse for lesson:

Beloved, I pray that you may prosper in all things and be in health, just as your soul prospers (3 John 2 NKJV).

THE ?ARADOXICAL JESUS in 3 JOHN

We know the Bible does not contradict itself, so it is important to take time to study and understand all sides of the truth and interpret Scripture in light of Scripture to grasp the whole truth as much as possible.

We read here that Diotrephes loved to be first, which goes against Jesus' teaching, "the first shall be last, and the last shall be first". From a worldly perspective, this seems to be a contradiction.

How does the Kingdom of God show this to be true when we look at the life of Christ?

___

I saw Jesus more clearly in this book when...

JESUS UP CLOSE:

LESSON 65

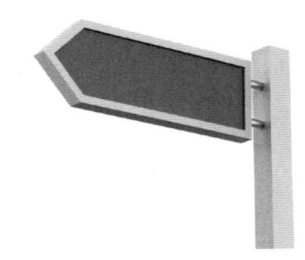

JUDE: GUIDE

In your SEEING JESUS Study Guide:
Read through the fast facts, author and setting, and overview on page 501 and 502. Reflect and take notes.

Jesus in Jude:

Jude's desiring was to keep Christians from falling. He warned against those smuggling in false teaching. He gives a strong denunciation against those in error. He also gives praise to God for His ability to keep the church and individuals from falling.

Read the book of Jude in one sitting. Circle words or phrases that speak of his guidance to the church.

Jude's message is short but strong: **STAND FIRM, GROW, AND CONTEND FOR THE FAITH.**

Jude - Persevere

Jude, a servant of Jesus Christ and a brother of James,

To those who have been called, who are loved in God the Father and kept for Jesus Christ:

2 Mercy, peace and love be yours in abundance.

The Sin and Doom of Ungodly People

3 Dear friends, although I was very eager to write to you about the salvation we share, I felt compelled to write and urge you to contend for the faith that was once for all entrusted to God's holy people. **4** For certain individuals whose condemnation was written about long ago have secretly slipped in among you. They are ungodly people, who pervert the grace of our God into a license for immorality and deny Jesus Christ our only Sovereign and Lord.

5 Though you already know all this, I want to remind you that the Lord at one time delivered his people out of Egypt, but later destroyed those who did not believe. **6** And the angels who did not keep their positions of authority but abandoned their proper dwelling—these he has kept in darkness, bound with everlasting chains for judgment on the great Day. **7** In a similar way, Sodom and Gomorrah and the surrounding towns gave themselves up to sexual immorality and perversion. They serve as an example of those who suffer the punishment of eternal fire.

8 In the very same way, on the strength of their dreams these ungodly people pollute their own bodies, reject authority and heap abuse on celestial beings. **9** But even the archangel Michael, when he was disputing with the devil about the body of Moses, did not himself dare to condemn him for slander but said, "The Lord rebuke you!" **10** Yet these people slander whatever they do not understand, and the very things they do understand by instinct—as irrational animals do—will destroy them.

11 Woe to them! They have taken the way of Cain; they have rushed for profit into Balaam's error; they have been destroyed in Korah's rebellion.

12 These people are blemishes at your love feasts, eating with you without the slightest qualm—shepherds who feed only themselves. They are clouds without rain, blown along by the wind; autumn trees, without fruit and uprooted—twice dead. **13** They are wild waves of the sea, foaming up their shame; wandering stars, for whom blackest darkness has been reserved forever.

14 Enoch, the seventh from Adam, prophesied about them: "See, the Lord is coming with thousands upon thousands of his holy ones **15** to judge everyone, and to convict all of them of all the ungodly acts they have committed in their ungodliness, and of all the defiant words ungodly sinners have spoken against him." **16** These people are grumblers and faultfinders; they follow their own evil desires; they boast about themselves and flatter others for their own advantage.

A Call to Persevere

17 But, dear friends, remember what the apostles of our Lord Jesus Christ foretold. **18** They said to you, "In the last times there will be scoffers who will follow their own ungodly desires." **19** These are the people who divide you, who follow mere natural instincts and do not have the Spirit.

20 But you, dear friends, by building yourselves up in your most holy faith and praying in the Holy Spirit, **21** keep yourselves in God's love as you wait for the mercy of our Lord Jesus Christ to bring you to eternal life.

22 Be merciful to those who doubt; **23** save others by snatching them from the fire; to others show mercy, mixed with fear—hating even the clothing stained by corrupted flesh.

Doxology

24 To him who is able to keep you from stumbling and to present you before his glorious presence without fault and with great joy— **25** to the only God our Savior be glory, majesty, power and authority, through Jesus Christ our Lord, before all ages, now and forevermore! Amen.

Reflection Exercises:

Jude warns against false teachings which have "crept in." From observation and thinking about your own experience, how do false teachings find a door or window to creep in, often unnoticed?

___

Jude first speaks to the common fellowship we have as believers, then charges the reader to contend for the faith. Think about all the heresies that have tried to plague the church in the past. What are some modern heresies that have tried to attach to the purity of the Gospel? Think about some modern-day cults.

___

Jude mentions the error of Balaam, though God allowed this seer to prophesy about the coming Messiah. What did Balaam represent in the way of false religion?

___

Jude and James were the two brothers of Jesus who wrote epistles in the New Testament.

Unpacking the Outline:

See the lesson outline for Jude on page 503 of your study guide

---

JUDE APPEALS IN HISTORY TO SHOW EXAMPLES OF APOSTASY IN JUDE 5-7

1. Cain, ignored the shedding of blood
2. Balaam, controlled by love of money
3. Korah, showed rebellion in the wilderness because of lust for power

How do these examples help us to discern from the past and how to watch out for false prophets today? Any pastor who denies the power of the Cross or the Resurrection, would be a false teacher. Read the Apostle's Creed, a creed from the 4th century declaring the orthodox teachings of Christianity.

1. I believe in God the Father, Almighty, Maker of heaven and earth
2. And in Jesus Christ, his only begotten Son, our Lord
3. Who was conceived by the Holy Ghost, born of the Virgin Mary
4. Suffered under Pontius Pilate; was crucified, dead and buried: He descended into hell
5. The third day he rose again from the dead
6. He ascended into heaven, and sits at the right hand of God the Father Almighty
7. From thence he shall come to judge the quick and the dead
8. I believe in the Holy Ghost
9. I believe in the holy catholic church (universal): the communion of saints
10. The forgiveness of sins
11. The resurrection of the body
12. And the life everlasting. Amen.

The early church established creeds as response to certain heresies rising. Which of these tenets are being challenged in the church today?

Focus: Central Verse / Passage
Read Jude 20-25

What special words of comfort does Jude give?

How do we build ourselves up in the faith?

___

Memory Verse for lesson:

Now to Him who is able to keep you from stumbling, And to present you faultless Before the presence of His glory with exceeding joy, **25** To God our Savior, Who alone is wise, Be glory and majesty, Dominion and power, Both now and forever. Amen (Jude 24-25 NKJV).

THE ?ARADOXICAL JESUS in JUDE

We know the Bible does not contradict itself, so it is important to take time to study and understand all sides of the truth and interpret Scripture in light of Scripture to grasp the whole truth as much as possible.

One of the greatest threats to the early church was Gnosticism, which denied that Deity could take on flesh. There was a belief that all the material world was evil. While we are to hate the world, we also know that Jesus died for the world and loves His Created order in the world. What is the difference between denying anything good from the material world and hating materialism?

___

I saw Jesus more clearly in this book when...

JESUS UP CLOSE:

NOTES

NOTES

NOTES

APPENDEX
LEADER'S GUIDE & ANSWER KEYS

LEADER'S GUIDE: INTRODUCTION

I'm so glad you decided to make the commitment to take a deeper look at Scripture using the *Seeing Jesus Bible Encounter Series Workbook*. Throughout my years of teaching the Bible, I find one of the most encouraging encounters we can have is to see Jesus, the Living Word, in the most surprising and unexpected places. Jesus Christ, the cornerstone of our faith, is the One we are to imitate and follow. Through this study, I know you will be encouraged by the power of the Word and actively see Jesus through the pages of both the Old and New Testament.

I want to warmly welcome you, dear friend, and leader of the group. I wish there was a way I could sit in on your study group and hear the stories around the table. In this volume, I know you will encounter many unexpected blessings that only Jesus can give you. You will have the opportunity to hear some of the insights from Scripture that God has revealed to me, and those you are studying with, and together, we will also see Jesus much more clearly. I'm very excited about this resource that supplements my, *Seeing Jesus Bible Encounter Study Guide*. The workbook and the study guide work well together and will reinforce your study. You may choose to do this as an independent learner or in a small group or church learning environment.

VOLUME 6 : LEADER'S GUIDE

The *Seeing Jesus Bible Encounter Series Workbooks* contain the following study material:

1. THE PENTATEUCH – VOLUME 1
2. HISTORY – VOLUME 2
3. POETRY / WISDOM BOOKS – VOLUME 3
4. MAJOR / MINOR PROPHETS – VOLUME 4
5. GOSPELS / ACTS & ROMANS – VOLUME 5
6. EPISTLES – VOLUME 6
7. END TIMES – VOLUME 7

You'll be amazed at the Jesus sightings we found throughout every volume. And our encounters with Jesus, I know, He will meet your you right where you are, as He is the Bread of Life. My prayer is this will move well past head knowledge to the heart, where faith can be lived out. With that, let's take a look at the format. Whether you are leading the group or leading yourself through this study, this will help acclimate you to the materials and be prepared to receive as much as you can as you look at each book of the Bible.

Study Format

The lessons will give you a key concept for each book to help you remember the focus of the book. The following sections are consistent throughout each volume, which include reflection exercises, scripture reading, memorization exercises, and practical application steps.

1. Jesus in (respective book name here)
2. Unpacking the Outline
3. Focus: Central Passage
4. Memory Verse for Lesson
5. Paradoxical Jesus
6. Jesus Up Close

These lessons are set up to work well in a 60-90 minute session, depending on the size of your group. Through these sections, you will have various opportunities to grab hold of the context and see where Jesus shows up. Don't rush! Enjoy these moments in the Word and invite Him to show you deep revelations that you could not grasp without the help of His Spirit (Jeremiah 33:3).

Group Study—Lesson 1
Your weekly group gathering will take around one and a half hours to complete. This will be a good length to plan for when you are using the study guide or engaging in the video lessons. The weeks when a video lesson applies, note that the video length is about **20 minutes**. Allow time for discussion and prayer.

Video
When there is a video lesson, use it as main focus for the study group. Summary points with fill-in-the-blank questions and some key concepts are included for you to complete as you follow along with the video.

Small Group Discussion
Following the video, you'll see a section of small group discussion questions. Let these questions guide you as you discuss God's promises with fellow believers. Learn from those who have been given different experiences with God's promises. Refer to the leader's guide for further supplemental material listed in subsequent pages.

Prayer
The group discussion time each week will conclude with a time of prayer. Through this study, I want to stress the importance of prayer as our lifeline to God's grace. Some participants in your group may be new to this type of setting, so be sensitive to where the comfort level of praying out loud might be. As a facilitator/leader, take the lead in making sure everyone is prayed for each week.

Start Up
As you have read over the introduction, I want to take a moment to specifically encourage you as one who will create an inviting environment for all the participants. I pray God uses your gifts to help facilitate this study. It is important for you to feel comfortable with the format and style so that you can answer questions and provide support as needed. While your responsibilities are mainly fulfilled in guiding everyone through the sections each time you meet, you may also want to make yourself available to participants throughout the week, whether it is for prayer support or direction in understanding the Scriptures.

Resources Needed
You will need a **DVD player** and a **room or facility** that is conducive to small group discussions. You may want to bring **extra Bibles** for those who may not have one or forget theirs. You may also wish to bring several translations of the Bible to the study. Encourage participants to raise questions and find answers together. Make a point to make everyone feel comfortable, connected, and allow participants the opportunity to share their insights when appropriate.

Prior to each session, take time to review your leader's guide to help focus your preparation for the coming lessons. You will find additional discussion questions and bonus information that may help create more interaction. I would encourage you to watch the video lesson segments prior to facilitating to sharpen your grasp of the material and as a way to prepare for the discussions.

Study Group Dynamics
Because of the types of study and reflection questions, I'd recommend that your breakout groups be no larger than three to five participants. This will offer some level of intimacy and the ability to answer any questions in greater depth. This will also cultivate a prayerful learning environment. You may want to monitor group discussions from a distance to assure participants feel comfortable in their groups. Encourage everyone to be open as they share answers to the discussion questions, but also not to be afraid of silence or giving a wrong answer. There are no wrong answers in group discussions and all are qualified to answer, whether the participant is a new believer or a seasoned Christian.

Leader's Role
I encourage you to be prepared with the weekly lesson prior to your day of study together. Read over the sections and fill in answers ahead of time. Reading the highlighted passages ahead of time will be a great way to anticipate questions and lead with more confidence. However, you do not have to speak through every part of the lesson. Avoid dominating the discussion with your own insights. Most of the deeper teaching moments will come from the group's reflections collectively.

Time Keeping
It will be up to you to move the groups along and keep things close to the suggested time allotment noted beside each lesson. Be respectful of schedules, offering closure at the time agreed upon so no one feels left out of prayer time at the end of each lesson.

For the first lesson, take a bit of time to introduce yourself. Share how you learned about the *Seeing Jesus* resource and what led you to host the group. Make sure everyone has a chance to become acquainted. You may have committed to studying all seven volumes, or perhaps just one volume. The study works well to add participants at any time, so welcome those who may join later. It is a study where anyone could easily begin at any week and finish missed sessions independently.

Video Segment
When it applies, make sure the technical equipment is set up in plenty of time so you can begin the DVD once everyone is ready. Some participants may miss the fill-in-the-blank answers, so point others to the answers supplied in the back of the study guide.

I'd encourage you to solicit feedback after the first session to make sure the setting met the needs of your participants.

ADDITIONAL STUDY NOTES

VOLUME 6 – THE EPISTLES
1 CORINTHIANS - JUDE

LESSON 46 – 1 CORINTHIANS

Warm-up exercise:
When you think of "church," what comes to mind? You might think of a building, but in Paul's time there were no buildings. Believers met in homes. It was like this for the next 200 years. Brainstorm some words that describe what the church body is.

- In 1 Corinthians, Paul explains how the Holy Spirit equips each Christian with abilities to minister to others (1 Corinthians 12).
- Paul was dealing with immature Christians in Corinth. He speaks against the quarreling that was happening and a list of other issues.

Bonus Question:
Paul deals with the sins of sexual immorality, selfishness, abuse in taking the Lord's Supper, and division. What sin do you think is most difficult to overcome today?

LESSON 47 – 2 CORINTHIANS

Warm-up exercise:
Paul loved the church, though sometimes his words seemed harsh. Proverbs 27:6 tells us that "the wounds of a friend can be trusted." When someone loves us, we know the truth is life-giving. When have you experienced this to be true?

- Paul opens acknowledging their repentant attitudes and willingness to correct the problems he addressed in his first letter.

VOLUME 6 : LEADER'S GUIDE

- 2 Corinthians 8 and 9 give the longest exposition in the Bible on generosity and giving.

Bonus Question:
Jesus doesn't emphasize the tithe in the New Testament, but rather radical generosity and cheerful giving. Share some stories how God has blessed faithful giving, even when it seems sacrificial. Then take some time to pray for those you know have real financial needs.

LESSON 48 - GALATIANS

Warm-up Exercise:
Paul was very upset to hear of the Christians in Galatia who were so easily swayed by the Judaizers. Though we don't grapple with trying to instill Jewish customs as a means of our salvation, how does legalism still sometimes creep in, particularly in the order of worship on Sunday?

- Paul reminds the Galatian Christians that they were saved by faith in Jesus Christ.
- Galatians 5:1 is a key passage in this book.

Paul clearly sets out to show the superiority of the Gospel over the Law of Moses.

Bonus Activity:
Galatia was a region in the Roman Empire, which is now Turkey. Take time to study a Bible study map on Paul's letters. See map A18 in the back of your study guide to see where Galatia is. You may wish to do some research on modern-day Turkey and discuss the modern context with the biblical context of Paul's day.

LESSON 49- EPHESIANS

Warm-up exercise:
As different parts of the body of Christ, Christians have different roles, but we should have a visible unity in working together. What are some of the most common ways unity is interrupted in the work of the church?

- One of Paul's themes in this letter is to show Christians how treasured they are by God. His love is limitless for us.
- Paul reminds believers that we are "in Christ", therefore we have a relational faith to live out.

The seven Ones in Ephesians (Ephesians 4:4-6):

One Body (church)

One Spirit

One Hope

One Lord

One Faith

One Baptism

One God

VOLUME 6 : LEADER'S GUIDE

Bonus Question:
Take a look at the seven Ones above. Assign 1-7 to a person or break up into small groups until all seven are covered. Have the person or group come up with a few sentences as to what it means to be "one Body" or have "one hope."

LESSON 50 – PHILIPPIANS

Warm-up Exercise:
Paul had been in jail in Philippi. In the miraculous act of God, his prison guard became a Christian as we read in Acts 16. This jailer became part of the Philippian church. When has a bad circumstance you've endured led to God doing something miraculous in the life of someone else?

- This letter is a combination of a thank you to believers and a letter of great encouragement.
- Paul emphasizes the joy we can have, despite circumstances.

Key points:
Consider suffering a privilege (Philippians 1:20-29); Be humble (Philippians 2:1-11); Recognize what is important (Philippians 3:7-11).

Bonus Question:
Turn to back of study guide to Map A16 to review Paul's first and second missionary journeys. Take time to look up the corresponding verses next to the cities. You may want to use a white board and list what the scriptures say about the various places Paul visited.

LESSON 51 – COLOSSIANS

Warm-up exercise:
Colossians is a book that takes us "back to basics." Take a moment and discuss some of the basics of Jesus' teachings that are the easy ones to forget. (i.e., love, forgiveness.) Discuss as a group before studying what Paul wrote.

- Colossians is one of the four prison epistles.
- Paul reminds the church that Christ is all that is needed for salvation.

Key passage:
Colossians 2:8-10

Bonus Question:
Some of the false teaching Paul addressed was the idea that Christianity wasn't sophisticated enough. They were teaching that intellectualism was the way to reach higher levels of spiritual understanding. In today's world, this might come up in the form of humanism, which places man's thinking, reason, and ability above God's. What are some ways we can be mindful to not fall prey to thinking our intellect is what God values more than our submission to Him?

LESSON 52 – 1 THESSALONIANS:

Warm-up exercise:
Paul speaks to the church to encourage them to stand firm in their faith. In what area of your life is God asking you right now to trust Him and stand firm?

Key verse:
"Test all things; hold fast what is good." –1 Thessalonians 5:21

Paul encourages:

- to increase in brother love
- to rejoice
- to pray
- to give thanks always

Bonus Question:
From the list above, which one do you believe God has given you an extra measure of grace to live out, despite circumstances? Share your thoughts.

LESSON 53 – 2 THESSALONIANS

Warm-up exercise:
2 Thessalonians is the last letter Paul writes to a congregation. If you were to write a letter to your congregation, knowing it would be the last words you could share, what would you say?

Paul established this church during his secondary missionary journey and stayed there for about two months.

Key verse:
"Do not grow weary in doing good." –2 Thessalonians 3:13

- Believers are to look forward and expect the return of Christ.

Bonus Question:
Paul's interest in the Thessalonian converts did not terminate with his first letter. He continued to have a heart to disciple and encourage them. Take a moment to think about those God has called you to encourage along in the faith. When have you persevered and seen God's faithfulness? When have you been convicted that you didn't follow through with a young believer?

LESSON 54 – 1 TIMOTHY

Warm-up exercise:
Paul instructs Timothy about qualities of leadership. What have you learned from strong leaders? What have you learned from bad leaders?

In 1 Timothy, Paul covers:

- worship
- criteria for church leaders
- warnings against false doctrine

Bonus Activity:
In 2 Timothy 4:6-7, Paul sort of writes his own epitaph. He intended to finish well for Christ Jesus, and he did. If you were to write your own epitaph, what would it say?

LESSON 55- 2 TIMOTHY

Warm-up exercise:
From our study so far, brainstorm as a group a list of characteristics that marks a "true" teacher. Contrast this list with a "false" teacher. Discuss your answers.

- Metaphors used: soldier, athlete, a farmer
- Paul is in prison, suffering along with hardened criminals. Yet he rejoices that the Word of God is not in chains.

Bonus question:
Self-discipline is a requirement of a Christian. Choose one the metaphors above to describe your own walk with Jesus. Share your summary with your group.

LESSON 56 - TITUS

Warm-up exercise:
To sum up Titus, character does count. Think about our nation's leadership over the years. Without getting into partisan discussions, go around and share which president you most admire and why. How does character come into play?

- Like Timothy, Titus was young and Paul encouraged him to hold to truth, as the Cretans were used to a culture of deception and lying to one another.
- Themes: character counts, follow sound teaching, and submit to civil authorities

Bonus Question:
Study the topic of civil disobedience. When do you think God approves of someone rebelling against the law? Do you think there is ever times when God would allow us to break the law? (i.e., smuggling in Bibles)

LESSON 57 – PHILEMON

Warm-up exercise:
Philemon is a challenging letter that addresses a Christian who owned a slave. Think about the United States and our history of slavery. Do you think it was ever right for Christians to own slaves when it was legal? What ills have we had to overcome because of our history with slavery?

- Forgiveness should be a natural occurrence in relationships between Christians.
- Philemon is one of four books that Paul addresses to specific individuals
- Onesimus was a common slave name; it meant "useful" or "profitable."

Bonus question:
Paul, Philemon, and Onesimus are persons in a real drama with social ramifications. A runaway slave, a slave owner, and the Apostle Paul have all encountered one another. All are from different walks of life. Think of a similar setting in the contemporary world where three men from various social standings might have to come together for the sake of the Gospel.

LESSON 58 – HEBREWS

Warm-up exercise:
The book of Hebrews was written to Christians who were Hebrew. In the Old Testament, the prophets, priests, and kings, filled in the roles of God's chosen people. Jesus came as a prophet, priest, and king as well. Discuss this truth for the Christian.

Key verse:
Hebrews 10:11-12

Contrasts in Old/New Covenant:

OLD	NEW
Moses/Mediate	Christ/Mediator
High Priest/Aaron	High Priest/Christ
Priests/Levites	Priests/Every believer
For Jews Only	For all nations

- The recipients of Hebrews probably lived in Rome
- this was written to teachers (5:12) and the author has a good opinion of his audience

Bonus question:
If you were to sit down with a Jewish friend today, what would you want to know about their faith? What would you want to share about yours?

VOLUME 6 : LEADER'S GUIDE

LESSON 59 – JAMES

Warm-up exercise:
James speaks against showing partiality. How do we show favoritism in the church, though often we don't realize it?

- James wrote to Jewish Christians who were living in the regions of Palestine.
- James and Jesus had the same mother, Mary.
- for a long time, James didn't believe that Jesus was the Messiah. Read this epistle with that in mind.
- book was written before AD 60

James speaks words that mark Jesus' sermon found in Matthew 5-7

Bonus question:
Our faith is often tested when we are under trials and God knows that well about humanity. What are some life lessons you would not have learned without persevering under trial?

LESSON 60 – 1 PETER

Warm-up exercise:
Think about Peter in the Gospels and some of the mistakes he made as a disciple. In what ways can you relate to Peter?

Peter was one of the first called into service for Jesus. He was a fisherman from Bethsaida. He was influenced by John the Baptist; his brother Andrew was a disciple of John the Baptist.

Key theme:
How do we live when the trials of life overwhelm

Bonus Question:
We know quite a bit about Peter from the Gospels and the book of Acts. What are some memorable things about Peter from your study? (walked on water, denied Jesus three times, he opened the doors to Jews and Gentiles (Acts 2; Acts 11). Why do you think Jesus built his church on Peter?

LESSON 61 – 2 PETER

Warm-up exercise:
Write down some memorable stories of Peter from the Gospels in a phrase or two. Play a game of charades, dividing your group in half.

- It's not known for sure where 2 Peter was written. Because Peter spent time in Rome, it is possible he wrote it there.

Peter stresses: faith, virtue, knowledge, self-control, perseverance, godliness, brotherly kindness, and love.

VOLUME 6 : LEADER'S GUIDE

Bonus Question:
Peter stresses that the prophecies given were not man's, but rather came from the will of God by His sovereignty. He says the prophets spoke and wrote as they were carried along by the Holy Spirit. How do Peter's words help us now to discern if a prophecy is carried along by the Holy Spirit or by man?

LESSON 62 - 1 JOHN

Warm-up exercise:
John also was in the inner circle with Jesus and Peter. Contrast John's personality with Peter's.

- John emphasizes lifestyle, not what someone knows about Christ
- stresses confession
- reader is pointed back to significance of John 1:1

Bonus Question:
John was the only disciple at the scene of the crucifixion with Jesus' mother, Mary. Why do you think John was the only one who showed up?

LESSON 63 - 2 JOHN

Warm-up exercise:
We've studied the effectiveness the epistles had on the early church. Think about a letter someone wrote to you that impacted you at a profound level. What made it particularly meaningful?

The Epistles were written during the first century AD after Christ's resurrection and ascension. They were written by Paul, Peter, and John. They gave instructions on how to become a Christian, how to mature in the faith, the importance of God's Word, and much more.

- elder can mean an old man, a senior person deserving respect, or a senior official of a local church
- heart of letter links truth and love together

Bonus question: What letter has been most impactful to you in the course of our study in the epistles?

LESSON 64 - 3 JOHN

Warm-up exercise:
The more you get to know God, the more you love Him. Share your experience in receiving more of God's love as you mature in your faith.

- John follows the theme of love in his third letter
- love means doing what God said

Bonus question:
According to what John says about love, do you think it is hypocritical to show a loving act to someone you don't like? Discuss.

LESSON 65 – JUDE

Warm-up exercise:
Discuss how you've recently seen someone defend their faith. How did it encourage you? Often we find it true that the purity of the Gospel is preached in times of persecution. As the leader, prep and do some research on the early martyrs of the church (i.e. Justyn Martyr, Polycarp.) Share their testimonies with the group and discuss how they defended the faith.

- Scripture references about Jude: Matthew 13:55; Mark 6:3; 1 Corinthians 9:5
- this is a letter of warning against smugglers in the church who bring in false teachings
- Jude refers to Michael, the archangel
- Jude was one of Jesus' brothers

Bonus question:
Jude insists that Christians need to grow in spiritual maturity so the faith can be protected, so the Word is not twisted. Go back to Matthew 4 and Jesus' temptations. How did Satan twist God's word? Have you experienced a leader in the church twisting the Word for personal motives? How can we safeguard against this?

ANSWER KEY

VOLUME 6 – THE EPISTLES

LESSON: 1 & 2 CORINTHIANS

1. Greece
2. Sanctifier
3. exhorter
4. giver
5. organizer
6. mercy

LESSON: GALATIANS & EPHESIANS

1. be free
2. captives
3. profitableness
4. Christ

LESSON: PHILIPPIANS & COLOSSIANS

1. think
2. power
3. Timothy
4. beloved
5. strengthens

LESSON: 1 & 2 THESSALONIANS

1. sinned
2. rule, reign

LESSON: 1 & 2 TIMOTHY

1. son
2. faithfulness
3. mentor, truth
4. revelation

LESSON: HEBREWS & JAMES

1. understand
2. God
3. obey

LESSON: 1 & 2 PETER & JUDE

1. grace, trial
2. word, grace
3. Satan, word
4. love, truth